THE ALASKA HOMEGROWN COOKBOOK

THE BEST RECIPES FROM THE LAST FRONTIER

WITH AN INTRODUCTION BY KIRSTEN DIXON

ALASKA
NORTHWEST
BOOKS®

Text © 2007 by Alaska Northwest Books®
Copyright to archival photographs as credited on page 224.
Illustrations © 2007 by Mindy Dwyer

Book compilation © 2007 by
Alaska Northwest Books®
An imprint of Graphic Arts Books
P.O. Box 56118
Portland, OR 97238-6118
(503) 254-5591

www.graphicartsbooks.com

Library of Congress Cataloging-in-Publication Data:

The Alaska homegrown cookbook : the best recipes from the last frontier.
      p. cm.
   Includes bibliographical references and index.
   ISBN 978-0-88240-857-6 (softbound)
   1. Cookery, American. 2. Cookery—Alaska. I. Alaska Northwest Books (Firm)

   TX715.A274 2007
   641.5973—dc22

                                    2007022853

Editor: Ellen Wheat
Designer: Elizabeth Watson
Illustrator: Mindy Dwyer

◄ THE LOUIS SPITZ FAMILY IN FRONT OF THEIR HOME IN RUBY.

Contents

Preface

We at Alaska Northwest Books are happy to continue a tradition started in 1963, when founder and publisher Bob Henning published the company's first cookbook about Alaska foods, *The Alaskan Camp Cook*. He described that effort as a labor of love, not just for the pleasure of sharing great recipes but for sharing Alaska and its natural bounty. Since that first cookbook some 40 years ago, each cookbook we have released has been more than a collection of recipes: each reflects the rich flavor and cultural heritage of Alaska as well as the independent spirit and welcoming nature of all Alaskans.

People everywhere gather to share food. In Alaska, sharing meant survival for our earliest residents. Today, sharing food among Alaska's indigenous peoples is a means of cultural survival as well. Many early homesteaders in the Northland lived far from stores, so they hunted, fished, gathered wild plants, and grew what vegetables they could to supplement the staples of flour, sugar, and canned goods they ordered in bulk and stored. Life was slower then, and there always seemed to be time to sit down with a visitor to trade stories over a cup of coffee and a slice of pie or a bowl of hot, steaming stew.

Sharing food in Alaska is still a cultural tradition. Many Alaskans today live much closer to stores now, but far from family, so gathering with friends for a meal is a way to soften solitude and to brighten long winters. Sharing recipes is also a continuing tradition. Alaskans are eager to find a new way to cook a freezer full of salmon or wild berries, or to prepare the giant zucchini and cabbages we grow here over the long summer daylight hours.

To create this collection of recipes, we pored over all of the cookbooks we have published since the beginning. Faced with thousands of recipes, it was no easy task to decide what to include. We focused on choosing foods—seafood, game, fruits, vegetables, baked treats—that are distinctively Alaskan or have become long-standing Alaska favorites. We picked a variety of recipes that have proven appeal to us and to others, including those that make our mouths water, those that are especially interesting from a historical or cultural perspective, and those that represent a modern fusion of Alaskan and international cuisines. We organized the book by type of food and/or by course. We retained the style and voice of each recipe from its original source to honor the author/editor and to reflect the character and times of that cookbook, so you'll find quite a mix of recipe presentations.

We have also gathered tidbits from the cookbooks and other books published by Alaska Northwest Books that address the culture of food in Alaska, and have sprinkled them throughout the pages of this book as sidebars. Those comments about food in the Northland from 40-plus years of publishing offer particular insights by Alaskans.

We want to thank all the contributors and authors of the cookbooks for their willingness to let us present their recipes in this new collection. Every attempt was made to contact each original contributor, but many of these cooks are no longer with us; we hope they will appreciate that a new audience is enjoying their recipes.

At the back of the book, we've included a source list of all the cookbooks used to complete *The Alaska Homegrown Cookbook*. If you find a recipe you like from one, you may want to add that book to your collection.

Compiling this book has been a trip down memory lane for me and for all of us involved. Some of the books predate my time with the company, but our editors and I helped conceive many of them and send them into the world, working closely with the authors who became like family to all of us. We are delighted to offer this new tribute to these great cooks and to continue the tradition of sharing good Alaskan food.

—Sara Juday
Associate Publisher

Introduction

KIRSTEN DIXON

Although I live at a wilderness lodge in a roadless area of Alaska, I own a small house in Anchorage—a kind of reverse cabin in the woods. This comfortable cottage offers refuge *to* civilization, a respite from rural Alaska lodge life so appreciated now and then— a trip to the bookstore or dinner out to a favored ethnic restaurant. It's here that I keep the majority of my coveted cookbook collection. I own hundreds of cookbooks, all carefully catalogued, organized by category, frequently referred to, and dearly loved. I am often in Anchorage during "freezeup and breakup," the times of year when airplanes can't fly in or out of our remote location. It's then that you can find me sitting cross-legged in front of a big pile of books, thumbing through pages, attaching small sticky tabs to mark where to find a particular recipe or passage or tip.

Of all of my books, my favorite collection is the shelf filled with Alaskan cookbooks. The majority of the sources used in this compilation are represented there. I can sit for hours, lost in the stories of the people who took the time to share their lives, their knowledge of living in Alaska, and the recipes that became important to them. These recipes aren't merely instructions on how to prepare food. They are living, interactive stories of how Alaskans have managed to define themselves through their cuisine. Each recipe in this collection sheds a bit of light on who we are as a people.

What is Alaskan cuisine? At first blush, it might seem that Alaska is too far off any culinary roadmap to be able to define a specific culinary style. But take a closer look, and you will find that we have a unique and vibrant food culture that reflects our natural world, our social and cultural history, our geographic place on the earth, and our values of self-sufficiency and independence.

Our Alaska native legacy is still reflected everywhere in daily life here—in our artwork, our clothing, and our social life. Many native communities still hold on to a vibrant heritage of consuming indigenous foods such as walrus and seal. You might not have access to foods such as walrus, (and, of course, marine mammals are now protected outside of Native populations) but the inclusion of these traditional recipes in this collection provides the

► THE KITCHEN PANTRY IN DICK PROENNEKE'S CABIN NEAR TWIN LAKES.

opportunity for authentic understanding and insight into Native culinary traditions.

Those who came in search of Alaska's rich natural resources, including fish, fur, and gold, left behind a legacy of food styles imported from their faraway homelands. Russian and Scandinavian influences are threaded throughout our local dishes. Early Russian residents brought cabbage and potatoes and other hearty northern garden crops to Alaska. Scandinavian fishermen brought pickled dishes and stews. We have many Asian influences in our dishes, which makes sense when you think about our geography and proximity to Asia.

Homesteader heartiness and endurance is reflected in many of the recipes in this collection. Look for clues to hardship in obtaining certain fresh ingredients in the crafting of some of the recipes: evaporated milk, canned lemon juice, and dehydrated onions make appearances for a reason. For many living in extreme, isolated conditions in the past (or even in the present), obtaining ingredients such as fresh milk or a fresh lemon was difficult or impossible. Baking breads, the use of sourdough, preserving and "putting by" foods for the root cellar, and gardening during our brief but glorious summers have all been important necessities to Alaskan homesteaders in the past, and many modern Alaskan cooks, me included, enjoy carrying on this tradition today.

With the longest coastline of any other U.S. state, we live amidst a thriving Pacific Ocean fishery. Alaskans are proud of our fishing heritage and strong modern commercial and sport-fishing industries. There is a wide range of seafood recipes represented in this collection, and I encourage you to try as many recipes as you can. All Alaska salmon are wild and considered "organic." The quality of our fish is so important to us, it is actually written into our state constitution that we won't allow farming of finfish within our boundaries. We have crab, halibut, shrimp, rockfish, and many other species of Pacific fish in abundance in our cuisine. Look around a little in Alaska and you will notice our iconic love of Alaska seafood in our art, on T-shirts, in books, on wind chimes, and even painted onto doormats. We revere our fish!

Into the land and away from the coast, highlights of our cuisine include wild berries, wild herbs and greens such as dandelions with blossoms, strawberry spinach, and mustard leaves, birds such as spruce grouse, ptarmigan, and geese, and game such as moose and

▶ A MAN AND LAMB IN A LOG CANOE IN KENAI LAKE.

caribou. Living off the land and utilizing the natural abundance around us has always been important to any good Alaskan cook.

Of course, Alaska isn't quite as remote and inaccessible as it was in the past. Our markets are replenished with the bounty of the Pacific Northwest and California daily by jet, we find Chilean and Australian fruit and meats in the markets in winter, and we can special-order products on the Internet. We have, still, a preference for the local in our cuisine. Thriving weekend farmers markets are emerging in most urban areas in the summertime, and gardeners are growing increasing portions of our market produce, much of it organic. Creative, talented young chefs are moving to the state and our ethnic populations are growing, exposing us to global delights, both in local restaurants and in ingredients found in stores.

In this diverse cookbook, you will find recipes that are simple and sophisticated written by authors who wrote from wilderness cabins by candlelight or from their professional urban kitchens. Some recipes are unobtainable glimpses into the past and a cultural tradition in transition. Many others are priceless additions to your own personal culinary collection. This book offers you an entire Alaska cookbook collection in one volume. I hope you, too, will get out your sticky tabs and make note of particular recipes or passages or tips. And when you prepare these recipes, you will feel connected to those who reached out to communicate their Alaskan lives and foodways with you.

The Andersons and their chickens.

Scrambled Morels and Eggs

The Alaskan Mushroom Hunter's Guide BEN GUILD

Sulphur polypore mushrooms may be substituted for morels for somewhat cheese-flavored scrambled eggs.

• Chop the mushrooms coarsely and sauté briefly in margarine. In a small bowl, beat the eggs until light; season to taste. Add the milk and beat again. Pour the egg mixture over the morels and stir gently just until the egg mixture is cooked. Serve with hot toast and wild strawberry jam.

1	cup morel mushrooms
2	eggs
2	tablespoons milk
	Margarine
	Salt and pepper

SERVES 1 OR 2.

Chive Speckled Eggs

Discovering Wild Plants JANICE J. SCHOFIELD

• Mix ingredients (except for flowers) well. Cook in greased skillet on medium heat, stirring constantly until set. Serve immediately, garnishing with chive flowers.

SERVES 3 TO 4.

6	eggs
3	tablespoons fresh chopped chives
3	tablespoons cottage cheese
2	tablespoons milk
3	chive flowers

Hazelnut-Crusted French Toast

A Cache of Recipes ∽ LAURA COLE

4 eggs
1 cup whole milk
¼ cup heavy cream
1 teaspoon vanilla extract
1 teaspoon almond extract
1 teaspoon ground cinnamon
¼ teaspoon ground cloves
¼ teaspoon ground nutmeg
2 cups coarsely chopped hazelnuts
10 thick slices of day-old French bread

This is an elegant way to serve French Toast. For a tropical-inspired dish, omit the spices and substitute 1 cup chopped macadamia nuts mixed with 1 cup shredded coconut for the hazelnuts.

• Preheat the oven to 425°F. (The oven needs to be at a true 400°F when the French Toast goes in. Ovens lose a huge amount of heat when the door is opened. It is important that the French Toast cooks quickly, keeping the interior moist while toasting the nuts.)

• Grease a sheet pan with margarine, or spray with nonstick cooking spray. Do not use butter; it will burn. In a wide, shallow bowl or pie plate, mix the eggs, milk, cream, vanilla extract, almond extract, cinnamon, cloves, and nutmeg. Place the nuts on a plate. Set 4 slices of bread in a bowl. Allow bread to sit for a few seconds to saturate it. Turn the bread to coat it completely. Dredge the soaked bread in the chopped nuts. Set the soaked bread on the sheet pan and repeat with the remaining bread.

• Reduce the oven temperature to 400°F. Bake for 10 minutes. Flip the bread and bake for 10 minutes more. Remove from the oven. The nuts should look toasted and the bread should be cooked all the way through. Serve with your favorite toppings.

MAKES 10 SLICES.

Ma Pullen's great pride was a Jersey cow, the only cow in that part of the world, and in the pantry stood the blue-enameled milk pans. The guest was given a bowl and a spoon and allowed to skim off cream for his porridge and coffee. Skimming your own cream at the Pullen House in the land of no cream was a ritual talked of all over the North in those days.

—*Two in the Far North,* MARGARET MURIE

Ya Sure Fish Breakfast

Life's a Fish and Then You Fry ∽ RANDY BAYLISS

Any Scandinavian worth his or her salt cod will eat fish to start the day. This is one of my favorites for an on-board breakfast. It's easy to make mass quantities for a large crew and can be cooked in one pot.

• Cut the potatoes into bite-sized pieces and place them in the bottom of a large pot of boiling water. Cut the fish fillet into 1-inch pieces and place them on top of the potatoes. When the boiling resumes, start your 10-minute clock. With 4 minutes to go on the clock, add two eggs to the boiling water. When the time is up, drain the potatoes and fish, put them in serving dishes, and break the soft-boiled eggs over them. Add a tablespoon of melted butter, grind some pepper for spice, and garnish with parsley. You betcha.

SERVES 1 VERY HUNGRY PERSON.

2	medium potatoes
2	eggs
4	ounces halibut or cod fillet
1	tablespoon melted butter

Pepper to taste
Chopped parsley

Fireweed Omelet

Cooking Alaskan ∽ RECIPE BY IVA SENT, as told to Mary J. Barry, "Camp Cookery, Trail Tonics, and Indian Infants," *Alaska Sportsman*, July 1964

• Steam young fireweed leaves until tender. Meanwhile, dice and fry some bacon, then add the drained greens and mix in two beaten eggs. Simmer for five minutes.

MAKES 1 OMELET.

Baked Eggs with Wild Mushrooms and Caramelized Onions

Wild Mushrooms ∿ CYNTHIA NIMS
(Northwest Homegrown Cookbook Series)

2 tablespoons vegetable oil
1 large onion, thinly sliced
¾ pound wild mushrooms, brushed clean, trimmed, and thinly sliced
Salt and freshly ground black pepper
4 eggs
¼ cup crème fraîche or whipping cream
Toast, for serving

A simple and savory way to start the day, this dish uses a nest of wild mushrooms and caramelized onions in which to bake individual eggs. To save time in the morning, you could prepare the caramelized onion-mushroom mixture the night before and refrigerate, covered.

● Preheat the oven to 400°F. Generously butter four 4-ounce ramekins or other small baking dishes.

● Heat the oil in a large skillet over medium heat. Add the onion and sauté it gently, stirring occasionally, until the onion is quite tender and just beginning to brown, about 10 minutes. Add the mushrooms and cook until the onion is nicely caramelized and the mushrooms are tender and any liquid they give off has evaporated, stirring often, 20 to 25 minutes longer. Season to taste with salt and pepper.

● Spoon the onion-mushroom mixture into the prepared ramekins, drawing up the edges slightly to make a nest for the egg. Break an egg into each ramekin and spoon 1 tablespoon of the cream over each egg, then season the tops lightly with salt and pepper. Put the ramekins in a baking dish, and pour boiling water into the dish to come about halfway up the sides of the ramekins. Bake until the egg whites are set and the yolks are still soft, about 15 minutes. Carefully lift the ramekins from the water and dry off the bottoms of the dishes, then set them on individual plates. Serve right away, with toast alongside.

MAKES 4 SERVINGS.

Sourdough Hotcakes, Basic Recipe

Alaska Sourdough ∾ RUTH ALLMAN

- Into the Sourdough Starter, dump sugar, egg, and oil. Mix well. Add soda the last thing, when ready for batter to hit the griddle. Dilute soda in 1 tablespoon warm water. Fold gently into Sourdough Starter. *Do not beat.* Notice deep hollow tone as sourdough fills with bubbles and doubles in bulk. Bake on hot griddle to seal brown. Serve on hot plates.

SERVES 2 TO 4.

Alaska Blueberry Sourdough Hotcakes

Alaska Sourdough ∾ RUTH ALLMAN

- To basic Sourdough Hotcake recipe above, add 1 cup fresh blueberries dusted with 2 tablespoons sugar. Let stand a few minutes. Fold gently into the batter just before adding the soda. Or, spoon the batter on the hot griddle. Sprinkle fresh blueberries over the top of the hotcakes. Bake until berries are cooked through. Turn. Serve on hot plates with maple sugar and sausages.

SERVES 2 TO 4.

2 cups Sourdough Starter (page 30)
2 tablespoons sugar
4 tablespoons oil
1 egg
½ teaspoon salt
1 scant teaspoon soda, or full teaspoon if starter is real sour

Then I got ready for morning. I uncovered the jar of sourdough starter, dumped two-thirds of it into a bowl, put three heaping teaspoons of flour back into the starter jar, added some lukewarm water, stirred and capped it. If I did this every time, the starter would go on forever.

—*One Man's Wilderness*, SAM KEITH FROM THE JOURNALS AND PHOTOGRAPHS OF RICHARD PROENNEKE

Russian America Blintz

Cooking Alaskan ∿ RECIPE BY RUTH ALLMAN, JUNEAU

Blintz Filling
2 cups dry
 cottage cheese
1 egg yolk
1 tablespoon sugar
2 teaspoons
 melted butter
2 teaspoons grated
 orange rind
¼ teaspoon cinnamon
Salt to taste
Blintz cakes, baked
 as directed
Garnish—sour cream or
 fruit

This creation, a specialty of Ruth Allman of the House of Wickersham in Juneau, is another variation of her Basic Sourdough Hotcakes.

• To the Sourdough Hotcakes basic recipe (page 15), add an extra egg. This will make batter very thin, as you want paper-thin 7-inch cakes. If you have time, allow the batter to rest from 1 to 3 hours before baking.

• Bake blintz cakes one at a time by pouring a small amount of batter into a hot, lightly greased 7-inch cast-iron skillet or crêpe pan. Tilt the pan quickly to spread the batter thinly and evenly over the bottom. Bake the cakes only on one side until blistered with bubbles and very lightly browned around the edges.

• To remove cakes from the pan, lift edges gently with a spatula, and the rest of the cake should peel away easily. Lay cakes, baked side up, in a single layer on a damp tea towel, or stack them with waxed paper between. Then you're ready to continue with Ruth's recipe.

• Mix filling thoroughly and then place a spoonful in the center of each blintz cake, on the baked side. Fold all four sides over the filling, envelope fashion, and seal with a dab of sourdough. At this point the blintzes may be held, chilled, in a covered dish, for several hours or overnight if you wish. When you're ready to serve them, place blintzes seam side down on a hot griddle (or a large skillet) greased well with equal parts butter and oil. Turn once to brown both sides. Serve immediately with sour cream or fruit.

SERVES 4 TO 6.

Sourdough Waffles, Basic Recipe

Alaska Sourdough ∿ RUTH ALLMAN

Into Sourdough Starter, dump sugar, egg, oil, and salt. Mix well. Dilute soda in warm water in jigger glass, stirring with your little finger. Fold soda gently into batter. *Do not beat.* Stir with easy rhythmic motion, turning the spoon. Notice the deep, hollow tone as batter thickens and doubles in volume with bubbles. Dip batter immediately to hot iron.

• Top a section of Sourdough Waffle with slab of ice cream. Douse with wild strawberries Dip chunk of Glacier Ice (sugar cube) into firewater (lemon extract), and set aflame! (Lemon extract will flame cold, whereas brandy must be heated to flame.)

SERVES 4 TO 6.

2	cups Sourdough Starter (page 30)
2	tablespoons sugar
4	tablespoons cooking oil
1	egg
½	teaspoon salt
1	teaspoon (scant) soda

Flaming Sourdough Waffle

Alaska Sourdough ～ RUTH ALLMAN

Created for the special celebration of Alaska statehood and raising of the forty-nine-star flag. Today it is served for tourists at the House of Wickersham, Juneau.

• Top a section of Sourdough Waffle with a slab of ice cream. Douse with wild strawberries. Dip chunk of Glacier Ice (sugar cube) into firewater (lemon extract), and set aflame! (Lemon extract will flame cold, whereas brandy must be heated to flame.)

SERVES 1.

1	section Sourdough Waffle (above)
1	slab Seward's Ice Box (ice cream)
Wild strawberries	
Sugar cube	
Lemon extract	

Brown, thin and light—nothing quite like a stack of sourdough hotcakes cooked over a wood fire in the early morning. I smeared each layer with butter and honey and topped the heap with lean bacon slices. While I ate I peered out the window at a good-looking caribou bedded down on the upper beaches. Now that's a breakfast with atmosphere!

—*One Man's Wilderness*, SAM KEITH FROM THE JOURNALS AND PHOTOGRAPHS OF RICHARD PROENNEKE

Crab and Leek Quiche

Crab ∾ CYNTHIA NIMS
(Northwest Homegrown Cookbook Series)

2 tablespoons unsalted butter

2 large leeks, white and pale green parts only, split, cleaned, and thinly sliced

Salt and freshly ground black pepper

8 ounces crabmeat

1½ cups grated Gruyère cheese (about 5 ounces)

3 eggs

1½ cups half-and-half

Pastry Dough

1½ cups all-purpose flour

½ teaspoon salt

½ cup unsalted butter, cut into pieces and chilled

4 to 5 tablespoons ice water, more if needed

The simple quiche has been taken to some extremes over the years but remains at its best when the eggs, cream, and cheese combine to cradle subtly flavored ingredients in a flaky crust. That's just what you'll find in this recipe: Gruyère is the cheese of choice (though Swiss is a nice alternative), with mildly oniony leeks embellishing the sweet crabmeat in the filling. This delicious quiche is an ideal option for breakfast, brunch, or lunch, or even as an appetizer.

• For the pastry dough, combine the flour and salt in a food processor and pulse once to mix. Add the butter pieces and pulse to finely chop the butter and create a mixture with a coarse, sandy texture. Drizzle the water into the dough, 1 tablespoon at a time, again pulsing briefly a few times just to blend in the water. It's important not to overmix the dough or it will be tough rather than flaky. The dough will not form a ball in the machine, but it has the proper amount of liquid if it feels neither dusty dry nor sticky when you squeeze some between your fingers. Turn the dough out onto the work surface, form it into a ball, and wrap it in plastic. Refrigerate the dough for at least 30 minutes before rolling it out.

• While the dough is chilling, melt the butter in a small saucepan over medium heat. Add the leeks and cook, stirring occasionally, until just tender, about 5 minutes. Season lightly with salt and pepper and set aside to cool.

• Preheat the oven to 400°F. Roll out the chilled dough on a lightly floured surface to a roughly 12-inch circle, and use it to line a 9- or 10-inch quiche or pie pan. Press the dough gently down the sides of the pan to be sure it is evenly covering the bottom. Using kitchen shears or a small knife, trim the outer edge of the dough to a ½-inch overhang, then fold that edge under and use your fingers to flute the pastry edge.

• Prick the bottom of the pastry shell with the tines of a fork, line the pastry shell with a piece of foil or parchment paper, and add pie weights or dry beans to cover the bottom. Bake the pastry shell until the edges are set, about 10 minutes. Take the pan from the oven, remove the foil and weights, and continue baking the crust until it is lightly browned and the bottom no longer looks raw, 3 to 5 minutes longer. (If the bottom of the shell starts to puff up, prick the dough again.) Take the crust from the oven and let cool slightly; reduce the oven temperature to 375°F.

• Scatter the sautéed leeks over the bottom of the pastry shell. Pick over the crabmeat to remove any bits of shell or cartilage, and arrange it evenly over the leeks. Finally, sprinkle the Gruyère over the crab. In a medium bowl, whisk together the eggs to blend, then whisk in the half-and-half with a good pinch of salt and pepper. Pour the custard over the quiche filling. Bake the quiche until the top is lightly browned and a knife inserted in the center comes out clean, 30 to 40 minutes. (If the pastry edge browns too quickly, loosely cover it with a strip of foil to avoid burning.) Let the quiche sit for about 5 minutes before cutting it into wedges to serve. The quiche can also be served at room temperature, though it needs to be refrigerated if you won't be eating it right away.

MAKES 8 SERVINGS.

Vegetable Quiche

Discovering Wild Plants ❧ JANICE J. SCHOFIELD

1 pie crust (see Pastry
   Dough, page 18)
4 eggs
1½ cups milk
1 teaspoon soy sauce
½ cup sharp cheddar
   cheese, grated
2 cups chopped wild
   greens (for example,
   geranium leaves,
   nettle leaves,
   dandelion leaves,
   shepherd's purse
   greens, peeled cow
   parsnip stems;
   adjust according
   to availability)

Place single pie crust in greased 9- or 10-inch quiche pan or pie plate. Preheat oven to 350°F. In bowl, beat eggs. Add milk and soy sauce and mix well. Stir in cheese and greens. Pour mixture into pie crust. Bake for 35 minutes, or until quiche is set and golden brown.

MAKES 6 TO 8 SERVINGS.

I needed a big wooden spoon to dip hotcake batter onto the griddle. One spoonful, one hotcake. In the woodpile I found scraps of stump wood that looked suitable. It took no more than an hour to turn out a good-looking spoon. The stove did a fine job on the hotcakes this morning and my wooden spoon is just right. Perfect-sized cakes every time.

—*One Man's Wilderness*, SAM KEITH FROM THE JOURNALS
AND PHOTOGRAPHS OF RICHARD PROENNEKE

▲ MRS. HAVEMEISTER WITH
HER CHILDREN IN GARDEN,
MATANUSKA VALLEY.

Sourdough Bread Pudding with Crab

Crab ∿ CYNTHIA NIMS
(Northwest Homegrown Cookbook Series)

Bread pudding shows up in a lot of guises these days, from the traditional after-dinner sweet to savory side dishes that accompany roast meats. This classic dish moves to the breakfast table in this variation, with tangy sourdough bread enveloping sweet crabmeat in an herby custard.

• Preheat the oven to 350°F. Generously butter a 9-by-13-inch baking dish.

• Scatter about half of the bread cubes evenly over the bottom of the baking dish, and sprinkle all but ½ cup of the cheese over the bread, followed by the onion. Pick over the crabmeat to remove any bits of shell or cartilage, and scatter the crab over the onion, then top the crab with the remaining bread cubes.

• In a medium bowl, whisk the eggs to blend, then whisk in the milk, parsley, and chives with salt and pepper to taste. Pour the egg mixture evenly over the bread and let sit for about 10 minutes, pressing the cubes down to help them evenly soak up the custard.

• Sprinkle the reserved cheese over the top and bake the bread pudding until the top is lightly browned and a knife inserted in the center of the dish comes out clean, about 45 minutes. If the top is well browned before the eggy custard is cooked, loosely cover the dish with a piece of foil. Let the bread pudding sit for a few minutes before cutting it into pieces to serve.

MAKES 8 SERVINGS.

1 small loaf day-old rustic sourdough bread (about 1 pound), cut into ½-inch cubes
2 cups grated cheddar cheese (about 8 ounces)
½ cup minced onion
12 ounces crabmeat
8 eggs
3 cups milk
2 tablespoons minced flat-leaf (Italian) parsley
1 tablespoon minced chives
Salt and freshly ground black pepper

Potato-Crusted Sausage Quiche

A Cache of Recipes ∾ LAURA COLE

Potato Crust

1 pound russet potatoes
1 egg
3 tablespoons all-purpose flour
½ teaspoon salt
¼ cup minced yellow onion
2 tablespoons butter, melted and divided

Filling

8 ounces bulk pork sausage
2 eggs
¼ teaspoon freshly ground pepper
1 cup evaporated milk
1 tablespoon all-purpose flour
1 clove garlic, minced
1½ cups grated cheddar cheese
1 tablespoon chopped fresh parsley

The potato crust helps make this a hearty and nutritious breakfast entrée. For a vegetarian version, substitute 1 cup lightly sautéed vegetables for the sausage.

• To make the potato crust: Preheat the oven to 350°F. Without peeling potatoes, grate them into a bowl of cold water. Swirl to release some of the starch. Pour the grated potatoes into a strainer, rinse well, and drain. Wring out any excess moisture with a clean towel, and transfer the potatoes to a clean bowl. Mix in the egg, flour, salt, and onion. Generously butter a 9-inch pie pan, using 1 tablespoon of the melted butter. Press the potato mixture into the pie pan, building up a rim on the sides, to form a crust. Bake for 15 minutes. Remove from the oven, brush the inside of the crust with the remaining melted butter, return to the oven, and continue baking for an additional 10 minutes.

• While the crust is baking, prepare the filling: In a heavy-bottomed skillet over medium-high heat, sauté the sausage until browned. Remove from the heat and drain off the fat. In a medium-size bowl, whisk together the eggs, pepper, milk, flour, and garlic.

• Spread the browned sausage on the bottom of the baked crust, sprinkle the grated cheddar cheese on top, pour the egg mixture over the cheese, and top with the chopped parsley. Return to the oven and bake for 30 to 40 minutes, until the center is set and the top is golden brown. Let cool and set for 10 minutes before cutting.

MAKES 8 SERVINGS.

Fish Potato Cakes

Cooking Alaskan ∽ RECIPE BY THE OLD
HOMESTEADER

A good breakfast or lunch for campers.

• Chop fish fillets very fine. Combine all ingredients except applesauce and fat and mix well. Place a well-greased heavy frying pan about 4 inches from hot coals, add fat and heat until fat is hot but not yet smoking. Drop fish potato batter by large spoonfuls onto hot pan; flatten cakes with spoon if necessary. Fry 3 to 4 minutes or until brown. Turn carefully and fry 3 to 4 minutes longer or until well browned. Drain on paper towels. Keep hot. Serve with applesauce.

MAKES 4 SERVINGS.

1   pound skinless
    fish fillets
3   eggs, beaten
2   tablespoons flour
2   tablespoons, or more,
    grated onion
1   tablespoon
    chopped parsley
1½ tablespoons salt
Dash of pepper
2   cups finely grated
    raw potato
Applesauce, warm
    or chilled
Fat, for frying

I climbed up past the hump and picked a two-pound coffee can of big, firm, dull red cranberries. I dumped them into a pan to cook them in their own juice. I stirred the berries around a bit and picked out the sticks, moss, and leaves. A fistful of sugar was next, followed with a shot of corn syrup, a few wooden spoonfuls of Mrs. Butterworth's syrup, and a generous spill of honey. Soon the potion was bubbling away. I mashed the plump berries with the spatula. When the mixture was cooled, I poured it off into empty bottles. Now those sourdoughs would have an elegant topping in the morning.

—One Man's Wilderness, SAM KEITH FROM THE JOURNALS
AND PHOTOGRAPHS OF RICHARD PROENNEKE

Young eskimo girl with blueberries.

Brown Sugar Oatmeal Muffins

The Winterlake Lodge Cookbook ⟶ KIRSTEN DIXON

Imagine that you are a winter guest at the lodge. It's a quiet, brisk morning and it is snowing heavily. You walk from your cabin to the lodge. A warm cup of coffee and a freshly baked oatmeal muffin are waiting for you. These delicious muffins are like enjoying a bowl of hot oatmeal in easy snack form. Add raisins, currants, or nuts if you wish.

- Preheat the oven to 400°F. Butter a 12-cup muffin tin.
- In a large bowl, combine the oats and buttermilk and let stand for about 1 hour. Add the eggs, brown sugar, and butter to the oat mixture, stirring until combined.
- Into a medium bowl, sift together the flour, salt, baking powder, and baking soda. Add the flour mixture to the oat mixture, stirring just until blended. Fill each muffin cup ¾ full with the oat batter.
- For the streusel topping, in a small bowl combine the flour and butter, mixing until mealy in texture. Add the brown sugar. Sprinkle some of the topping on each muffin.
- Place the muffin tin on the center rack of the oven. Bake the muffins for about 12 minutes, or until golden and a toothpick inserted into the center of a muffin comes out clean.

MAKES 12 MUFFINS.

1⅓ cups old-fashioned oats
1⅓ cups buttermilk, slightly warmed
2 eggs, lightly beaten
⅔ cup firmly packed light brown sugar
⅔ cup butter, melted and cooled
1⅓ cups flour
1 teaspoon salt
1½ teaspoons baking powder
¼ teaspoon baking soda

Streusel Topping
¼ cup flour
¼ cup butter at room temperature
2 tablespoons brown sugar

Jean's Rich Blueberry Muffins

Baked Alaska ∾ SARAH EPPENBACH

2 cups all-purpose
   flour
1 tablespoon
   baking powder
1 teaspoon salt
¼ cup vegetable
   shortening
⅓ cup sugar
2 eggs
⅔ cup milk
1 cup fresh blueberries

Muffins aren't just for breakfast in Alaska. Vehicles for whatever berries might be in season, they round out the contents of lunch boxes, picnic hampers, backpacks. A friend from Fairbanks keeps a basket of fresh muffins on the kitchen counter at all times, for noshing.

Jean Rogers, a Juneau children's book author and accomplished baker, likes to put these muffins in the oven so that they emerge just in time for dessert. Her dinner guests eat them piping hot and slathered with butter, scraping the papers for the last crumbs. She also makes a "guilt-free" version, using margarine and undiluted fat-free evaporated milk.

● Heat oven to 400°F. Grease a 12-cup muffin tin or line the tin with papers.

● Sift the flour with the baking powder and salt, and set aside. Cream the shortening with the sugar until light and fluffy, then add the eggs and milk and beat lightly. Stir in the dry ingredients, then the blueberries, mixing only enough to distribute the berries. The batter will be quite stiff.

● Fill the muffin cups ⅔ full and bake 20 to 25 minutes. The papers will stick a bit when the muffins are hot but will peel off cleanly when cool (if you can wait that long).

MAKES 12 MUFFINS.

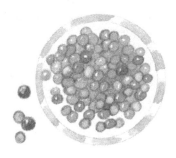

Rhubarb Muffins

Cooking Alaskan ᕦ **RECIPE BY MARTHA THOMAS,**
Second place, 1980 Tanana Valley Fair Bake-Off,
Bake-Off Cookbook, 1961–1980, Fairbanks

- Beat together brown sugar, oil, egg, vanilla, and sour milk. Add rhubarb and walnuts.
- In a separate bowl mix flour, soda, baking powder, and salt. Add to liquid ingredients, stirring only until moistened. Spoon into greased and floured muffin cups.
- For topping, mix all ingredients together. Scatter over filled cups and lightly press into the batter.
- Bake at 400°F for 20 to 25 minutes. Test with a toothpick for doneness.

MAKES ABOUT 20 LARGE OR 30 MEDIUM MUFFINS.

ᕦ *Note: If you don't have sour milk on hand, you can make it by stirring in 1 tablespoon of either vinegar or lemon juice per 1 cup of milk. Let stand for a few minutes.*

1½ cups brown sugar
½ cup oil
1 egg
2 teaspoons vanilla
1 cup sour milk (see Note)
1½ cups diced rhubarb
½ cup walnuts
2½ cups flour
1 teaspoon soda
1 teaspoon baking powder
½ teaspoon salt

Topping
2 teaspoons melted butter
⅔ cup sugar
1 teaspoon cinnamon

Lemon Cream Scones

A Cache of Recipes ⌒ LAURA COLE

Scones

2   cups of all-purpose flour
⅓   cup sugar
1   tablespoon baking powder
¼   teaspoon salt
¾   cup chopped fresh apricots (or ⅓ cup chopped dried apricots)
1   tablespoon grated lemon zest
1¼ cups heavy cream

Topping

1   tablespoon grated lemon zest
2   tablespoons sugar
3   tablespoons butter, melted

Try these with strawberry jam.

- To make the scones: Preheat the oven to 375°F.
- In a large bowl, combine the flour, sugar, baking powder, and salt. Add the apricots and lemon zest, and mix well. Slowly add the cream, mixing just until a dough forms. Turn out onto a lightly floured surface, roll out to the desired thickness, and cut into the desired shapes. Transfer to a sheet pan lined with parchment paper.
- To make the topping: Mix together the lemon zest and sugar. Brush the tops of the scones with melted butter. Sprinkle the lemon sugar over the scones.
- Bake for 15 to 20 minutes. The scones will be light golden brown. Serve warm.

MAKES 12 SCONES.

Saturday was baking and cleaning day.
When I was nine and a half, during that first winter in Fairbanks, I made my first batch of molasses cookies. After that nearly every Saturday morning found me making cookies. Mother baked pies, many of them, and doughnuts. These were put out into the cache or the screen porch and frozen, the same as the meat and the fish, and the many loaves of bread. All over town the women would be doing the same kind of thing.

—*Two in the Far North*, MARGARET MURIE

Cheddar Cheese Popovers

The Riversong Lodge Cookbook ∿ KIRSTEN DIXON

I love to make these popovers when I am having an especially busy breakfast. They are quick and easy and everyone loves them. Steam causes the batter to rise the way it does.

• Preheat the oven to 450°F. Generously grease the popover pans or regular muffin cups (popovers can be difficult to remove if they stick), and preheat them. Beat all the ingredients together until just smooth. Don't overbeat the mixture.

• Fill the prepared pans one-half to two-thirds full. Bake on the center rack of the oven for 15 minutes. Reduce the temperature to 350°F without opening the oven door. Bake until the popovers are firm and golden brown, 15 to 20 minutes more. Carefully remove the popovers to a linen-covered basket and serve warm with butter and jam.

1	cup all-purpose flour
¼	teaspoon salt
1	cup whole milk
⅔	cup shredded cheddar cheese
1	tablespoon unsalted butter, melted
2	eggs

MAKES 8 TO 12 POPOVERS.

Sourdough Bread

Alaska Sourdough ∿ RUTH ALLMAN

• Make soft sponge mixing the Sourdough Starter, water, sugar, oil, and salt. Add half the flour. Set in warm place to double in bulk.

• Add remainder of flour to make dough that is easy to handle, smooth and elastic. Place in greased bowl. Cover. Let rise in warm place until double in bulk.

• Knead down. Let rise to double in bulk.

• Form into loaves or roll out ¼ inch thick. Roll lengthwise and place on cookie sheet. Slash. Bake 500°F for 10 minutes, then 400°F for 45 minutes.

4	cups Sourdough Starter (page 30)
2	cups warm potato water
½	cup sugar
6	tablespoons cooking oil
1	teaspoon salt
10	cups flour, approximately

Basic Sourdough Starter

Alaska Sourdough ᥫ RUTH ALLMAN

Simple Method

1 cup active
  Sourdough Starter
2 cups water—rich
  potato water
2 cups flour
2 tablespoons sugar

Your Own Sourdough Starter

2 cups thick
  potato water
2 tablespoons sugar
2 cups flour
  (more or less)
½ teaspoon yeast
  (optional; use
  yeast only to
  speed action)

It is imperative never to use any metal pot or metal spoon with sourdough, as it causes a chemical action. A wooden spoon is a must to go with the sourdough pot—a crock or jar.

Simplest method:

• Obtain a cup of Sourdough Starter from an active working sourdough pot. Even a "smidgen of a cup" of starter will get the busy little enzymes working to build up a bubbling sourdough pot. Dump starter in a jar or crock to be used as the sourdough pot. Add the potato water, flour, and sugar (approximate proportions).

• Salt is omitted for it retards the action. Sugar used to speed up action—not to sweeten—and brown the sourdough.

Now, in case there is no Sourdough Starter available, just start your own. It's fun! It's easy!

• In pot, boil 2 medium potatoes with jackets on until they fall to pieces. Lift skins out and mash potatoes making a puree. Cool. Add more water to make sufficient liquid, if necessary. Richer the potato water, richer the starter. Put sugar, flour, and yeast in the pot with the potatoes. Beat until a smooth, creamy batter. Put in a crock or jar and cover. Set aside in warm place to start fermentation. Sourdough works best when the room temperature is between 65°F and 77°F.

Just how long does it take the Sourdough Starter to become "ripe"—in prime working condition? Exponents differ.

• 3-Day Starter: Sourdough Starter can be used now, providing those little enzymes have started working. But it is better to wait a few more days. Toss in extra fuel for the sourdough to work on—a spoonful of sugar along with a couple spoonsful of flour. Add water if batter is too thick. Mix well. Cover. Put in warm spot to work more.

• 1-Week Starter: Starter is now effervescing with a million bubbles. Looks like sour cream, smells like sour cream, but is rich, luscious Sourdough.

- **2-Week Starter:** Disciples of sourdough claim that waiting this extra time gives extra flavor, which is not to be compared with any other batter.
- **3-Week Starter:** The Sourdough Pot is now bubbling like the old witch's cauldron.
- **1-Month Starter:** Sourdough is now a rich, creamy batter that is honeycombed with bubbles.
- **1-Year Starter:** Old-timers claim a year must elapse before the sourdough matures and offers the distinctive taste appeal nothing else can imitate—Sourdough!

Note: For those wanting more information on the history of sourdough, making and keeping sourdough, and cooking with sourdough, see Alaska Sourdough *and* Cooking Alaskan.

Nature made it impossible for fruit trees to grow in the North. But she compensated for this with the most lavish gift of berries, and in those early times, because fresh fruit from the States was so rarely seen and more costly than jewels, it was necessary for each household to put up berries for the winter. Right after the Fourth of July celebration the picking began, blueberries first. Walking out from town in almost any direction in the open tundra you came to blueberries. Mother made blueberry pie, blueberry muffins, blueberry cobbler, blueberry syrup for the sourdough pancakes. We ate bowls of blueberries with canned milk and sugar on them. But more than all this, they must be put up for the winter. Berries and sugar were put in a 50-pound butter barrel—a layer of berries, a layer of sugar, and so on clear to the top. The best scheme for this project was to go out to some friend's on the creeks and spend three days picking the berries and packing them out there. Then you put them down in one of the mineshafts, where it was very cold. When winter came, the friend brought the barrel in and you put it in your own cellar under the kitchen, and all was well. A quart measure dipped into the barrel brings up a quart of juicy berries, almost like fresh ones.

—*Two in the Far North,* Margaret Murie

Basic Sourdough Biscuits

Cooking Alaskan ⌇ RECIPE BY THE OLD
HOMESTEADER

Sponge

½ cup Sourdough
    Starter (page 30)
1 cup lukewarm water
1 cup all-purpose flour

Biscuits

1½ cups all-purpose
    flour, to be added
    in two portions
¾ teaspoon salt
1 tablespoon sugar
1 teaspoon
    baking powder
½ teaspoon
    baking soda
1 tablespoon
    cooking oil
1 tablespoon
    margarine, melted
2 tablespoons corn
    meal (optional)

Set the sponge by mixing the following ingredients in a large
bowl. Cover it loosely with a foil or waxed paper lid and allow the
mixture to work overnight in a warm place.

When you are ready to bake, assemble these ingredients:

• Beat 1 cup of the flour into the sponge that has been working overnight (or at least 6 to 8 hours). In a small bowl combine
the remaining ½ cup flour with the salt, sugar, baking powder,
and soda, and sprinkle this mixture over the dough. Blend quickly
with a fork.

• Turn dough onto floured board and knead lightly about
10 times or until it is springy. Roll out to ½-inch thickness. Cut
with a biscuit cutter (a can with both ends cut out makes a good
one) and dip in a mixture of oil and margarine. If you wish, sprinkle half of the optional corn meal in bottom of baking pans and
the rest on the top of the biscuits.

• Place biscuits in pan close together. Cover with a clean cloth
and set in a warm, draft-free place to rise until doubled in bulk,
30 to 40 minutes. Bake at 375°F until golden brown, about 25
minutes.

MAKES A BAKER'S DOZEN GOOD-SIZED BISCUITS.

A group of "sourdoughs" were the first known
climbers to summit the North Peak of Mount McKinley in 1910.
Their high-altitude food supplies included bacon, beans, flour, sugar,
dried fruits, butter, coffee, hot chocolate, and caribou meat.

—*To the Top of Denali*, BILL SHERWONIT

Sourdough Soft Ginger Cookies

Alaska Sourdough ~ RUTH ALLMAN

• Cream sugar and shortening. Add molasses, egg, and orange rind. Mix in sourdough. Add dry ingredients. Use enough flour to make soft dough. Chill the dough. Roll out on floured board. Cut. Bake on greased cookie sheet 375°F 10 minutes.

MAKES ABOUT 4 TO 6 DOZEN COOKIES.

½ cup sourdough
½ cup black strap molasses
½ cup shortening
¾ cup sugar
1 egg
3½ cups flour, more or less
2 teaspoons ginger
2 teaspoons cinnamon
1 teaspoon cloves
½ teaspoon cardamom
2 teaspoons grated orange (lemon) peel
1 teaspoon soda

◀ KARL EID, A FORMER OLYMPIAN, SKI JUMPING COACH, AND PASTRY CHEF, MAKING CHOCOLATES AT SPENARD PIGGLY WIGGLY, ANCHORAGE.

Judy Cooper's Chocolate Chip Oatmeal Cookies

Baked Alaska ∽ SARAH EPPENBACH

1½ cups all-purpose
    flour
1   teaspoon
    baking soda
1   teaspoon salt
1   cup vegetable
    shortening
1   cup brown sugar
1   cup granulated sugar
1   extra-large egg
3   tablespoons
    hot water
1   teaspoon vanilla
    extract
3   cups rolled oats
2   cups (12 ounces)
    semisweet
    chocolate chips

On Sunday evenings our dear friend and neighbor Judy Cooper would climb the many stairs to our house for the 9 P.M. broadcast of *Masterpiece Theater*, accompanied by a small contingent of her red Siberian huskies. Often she would bring dessert: depending on the season, a blueberry or rhubarb pie, or a brown paper bag of chocolate chip cookies hot from the oven.

These cookies have succored hundreds of Alaskans during Judy's 25-plus years in Alaska as a VISTA volunteer, recreation director, trans-Alaska pipeline laborer, artist, musher, kennel owner, and environmentalist. They have launched innumerable late-night ferry departures, energized skiing and hiking expeditions, sustained board meetings, and been auctioned at art and charity events. They're the best.

• Preheat the oven to 375°F

• Sift or stir together the flour, baking soda, and salt, and set aside. Cream the shortening and sugars until fluffy and light, then mix in the egg, hot water, and vanilla. Stir in the dry ingredients, followed by the oats and chocolate chips, and drop the dough by spoonfuls onto ungreased baking sheets. Bake 8 to 10 minutes, until the cookies brown and flatten. Cool on the baking sheets a couple of minutes before removing.

MAKES 5 DOZEN COOKIES.

∽ *Variation: Substitute 2 cups raisins or 1 cup raw sunflower seeds and 1 cup raisins for the chocolate chips.*

Sour Cream Cranberry Chocolate Cookies

The Winterlake Lodge Cookbook ⟶ KIRSTEN DIXON

These delicious cookies are soft, light in color, and very pretty. You may use any dried fruit, and if you are lucky enough to have dried blueberries where you shop, you should try them in this recipe. We use bittersweet chocolate, but you may certainly use semisweet or white chocolate if you prefer, or even try the recipe without any chocolate.

- Preheat the oven to 350°F. Butter a baking sheet.
- In a medium bowl, combine the flour, baking soda, salt, and nutmeg.
- In the bowl of a heavy-duty electric mixer fitted with the paddle attachment, beat together the butter and sugar. Add the vanilla and egg and blend until smooth. Add the sour cream alternating with the flour mixture. Remove the bowl from the mixer and with a large wooden spoon stir in the cranberries, the chocolate, and the pecans.
- Drop tablespoons of the cookie dough onto the prepared baking sheet, about 2 inches apart. Bake the cookies for about 10 to 12 minutes, or until they are golden brown. Remove the cookies and place them on a rack to cool.

MAKES ABOUT 3 DOZEN COOKIES.

2½ cups all-purpose flour
½ teaspoon baking soda
½ teaspoon salt
½ teaspoon grated nutmeg
8 tablespoons butter, at room temperature
1 cup sugar
1 teaspoon vanilla
1 egg
1 cup sour cream
½ cup chopped dried cranberries
½ cup chopped bittersweet chocolate
1 cup coarsely chopped pecans

Blueberry Bars

The Winterlake Lodge Cookbook ～ KIRSTEN DIXON

2¼ cups flour
1   cup sugar
1   cup chopped
    black walnuts
1   cup butter at
    room temperature
1   egg
1½ cups Homemade
    Fresh Blueberry Jam
    (page 197)

In any wilderness lodge repertoire, it is essential to have lots of cookie recipes, coffee cake and other snack cake recipes, and some good bar cookie recipes. This recipe is so quick and easy we can start it when guests depart from Anchorage for Winterlake and have them out of the oven and onto the coffee bar by the time they arrive. I make blueberry jam every late summer and fall, when the lodge is surrounded by plump berries.

- Heat the oven to 350°F. Butter an 8-inch-square baking pan.
- To make the crumb mixture for the bottom and the top of the bars, combine the flour, sugar, walnuts, butter, and egg in the bowl of a heavy-duty electric mixer fitted with the paddle attachment. Beat the mixture at a low speed until the mixture is crumbly, about 2 minutes. Set aside 2 cups of the crumb mixture.
- Press the remaining crumb mixture into the bottom of the baking pan. Spread the blueberry jam over the crumb crust, leaving about a ½-inch edge free of jam. Sprinkle the reserved crumb mixture evenly over the top of the blueberry jam. Press the crumb mixture lightly into the blueberry jam.
- Place the baking pan in the center of the oven and bake for about 35 to 40 minutes, or until the crumb topping is browned. Remove from the oven and cool completely. Cut the bars into 2-inch squares.

MAKES ABOUT 24 BARS.

Strawberry Rhubarb Bars

Cooking Alaskan ~ **RECIPE BY DENISE BALLIET,**
First-Place Winner, 1979 Tanana Valley Fair Bake-Off,
Bake-Off Cookbook, 1961–1980, Fairbanks

- Mix 1¾ cups flour and powdered sugar in a bowl. Cut in butter until mixture resembles coarse crumbs. Press mixture into greased 13-by-9-inch baking pan. Bake at 350°F until golden, 10 to 12 minutes.
- Mix sugar, ¼ cup flour, and salt in a large bowl. Lightly beat egg yolks. Stir egg yolks and cream into sugar mixture. Stir in rhubarb, strawberries, and lemon juice. Spread mixture evenly over crust. Bake until firm at 350°F, about 1 hour.
- Beat egg whites in a large mixer bowl until foamy. Beat in ½ cup sugar, 1 tablespoon at a time, until stiff peaks form. Spread over rhubarb mixture. Bake until light golden brown, 10 to 15 minutes. Cool in pan on wire rack. Cut into bars.

MAKES 24 BARS.

1¾ cups flour
2 tablespoons powdered sugar
½ cup butter or margarine
1½ cups sugar
¼ cup flour
¼ teaspoon salt
6 egg yolks
1 cup whipping cream
4 cups shredded fresh rhubarb
1 cup sliced strawberries
½ teaspoon lemon juice
6 egg whites
½ cup sugar

We made coffee and I felt privileged to be with such fine company. I had regretted losing my other companions, but these folks were fearlessly honest. Here we were away from outsiders, volunteers, and the media. We could confess our mistakes, share both our doubts and tidbits of hard-won wisdom. Food was a big subject. Lesley confessed to living on M&Ms and salmon strips, while Karen brought out a cheesecake bar that was perfect for the Iditarod. I had been chewing on rock-hard energy bars at the high risk of breaking a tooth. Strangely, Karen's treat did not freeze.

—*Running with Champions,* LISA FREDERIC

Riversong Lodge Fudge Brownies

The Riversong Lodge Cookbook ⌇ KIRSTEN DIXON

1 cup unsalted butter
3 ounces unsweetened chocolate
3 cups sugar
5 eggs
1½ cups all-purpose flour
2 cups coarsely chopped pecans
2 ounces bittersweet chocolate, chopped
2 ounces milk chocolate, chopped

We make brownies nearly every day at the lodge in the summer, then wrap them individually in plastic wrap and include them in river lunches. In the winter, our brownies sit on a large platter near the coffeepots.

• Preheat the oven to 350°F. Grease and flour a 13-by-9-by-2-inch baking pan.

• Melt butter and the unsweetened chocolate in a small, heavy-bottomed saucepan over low heat. Set aside.

• Beat the sugar and eggs in a large mixer bowl on high speed for 10 minutes. Beat in the melted chocolate mixture on low speed. Add the flour, mixing just until blended. Add the nuts and the chopped chocolate, mixing well.

• Pour the mixture into the prepared baking pan. Bake on the center rack of the oven until the center of the brownies is firm to the touch and a toothpick inserted comes out clean, about 35 to 40 minutes. Cool the brownies and cut into squares.

MAKES 32 BROWNIES.

Lemon Pound Cake with Fresh Berries

Baked Alaska ∾ SARAH EPPENBACH

When pie or cobbler seems too much dessert and sorbet too little, this light and lemony yogurt pound cake makes the perfect foil for Alaska's summer berries. For a richer, even more magnificent cake, use 6 eggs instead of 4 eggs.

- Preheat the oven to 375°F. Grease and flour tube or bundt pan.
- Sift together the flour, baking soda, and salt and set aside. Cream the butter until light; gradually add the sugar, and cream the mixture until light and fluffy. Beat in the eggs one at a time, then add the lemon juice. (The batter may curdle slightly but will smooth out during the next step.) Blend in the yogurt alternately with the dry ingredients, followed by the lemon zest.
- Pour the batter into the prepared pan and bake for 45 minutes to 1 hour or until the cake tests done with a wooden toothpick. Cool for 10 minutes in the pan before inverting onto a rack. When completely cool, dust the cake with powdered sugar. Cut into slices and serve with the berries and a spoonful of Fresh Raspberry or Strawberry Sauce.

MAKES 10 TO 12 SERVINGS.

∾ *Variation: Instead of dusting the cake with powdered sugar, make a tart lemon glaze by stirring together 2 tablespoons lemon juice and ¾ cup powdered sugar. Drizzle the glaze over the cooled cake.*

3 cups cake flour, stirred before measuring
1 teaspoon baking soda
¼ teaspoon salt
1 cup butter
2 cups sugar
4 eggs
2 tablespoons lemon juice
1 cup plain yogurt
1 tablespoon grated lemon zest
Powdered sugar, for dusting
About 3 cups mixed fresh berries, sweetened to taste, for serving
Fresh Raspberry or Strawberry Sauce for serving (page 206)

Harvest (Carrot) Cake

Cooking Alaskan ~ RECIPE BY BERNICE KINNEY,
An entry for the Tanana Valley Fair Bake-Off,
Bake-Off Cookbook, 1961–1980, Fairbanks

1¼ cups salad oil
2 cups sugar
2¼ cups sifted flour
2 teaspoons
   baking powder
1 teaspoon soda
½ teaspoon salt
1 teaspoon cinnamon
4 eggs
3 cups finely grated
   carrots
Cream Cheese Frosting

Cream Cheese
Frosting
¼ cup butter
4 ounces cream cheese
2 cups sifted powdered
   sugar
½ cup chopped pecans
   or walnuts

● Combine sugar and oil; mix well.

● Sift dry ingredients together, then add half to sugar mixture and blend. Add remaining dry ingredients alternately with eggs, mixing well after each addition. Stir in carrots. Pour into lightly oiled 10-inch tube pan and bake at 325°F for 70 minutes. Or, pour into three 8-inch layer cake pans and bake at 350°F for 25 to 30 minutes. (Double the frosting recipe for a layer cake.)

● Cream all ingredients together. Add enough milk to spread easily.

MAKES 12 SERVINGS.

Kate's Apple Snack Cake

Baked Alaska ～ SARAH EPPENBACH

Northern bakers tend to collect apple recipes, as might be expected—any fruit that travels well, keeps beautifully, tastes wonderful raw, and can be baked into a variety of delicious goods deserves unlimited space in the recipe box. My sister, Kate, gave me this recipe for hearty, eat-out-of-your-hand apple cake. You can vary the spices to suit your mood. I often add cinnamon or cardamom. Snack cakes like this don't need to be frosted—at most, a quick dusting of powdered sugar does the job.

• **Preheat** the oven to 350°F. Grease and flour a 9-by-13-inch baking pan.

• **Sift** the flour, sugar, baking soda, salt, allspice, and nutmeg into a large mixing bowl.

• **In another bowl,** lightly beat the eggs, then beat in the oil and vanilla. Stir the mixture into the dry ingredients. Add the diced applies, raisins, and nuts and mix thoroughly; the batter will be very stiff. Turn the batter into the pan and bake 50 to 60 minutes or until the cake tests done with a wooden toothpick. Cool and dust with powdered sugar.

MAKES 12 SERVINGS.

2	cups all-purpose flour
1½	cups sugar
1	teaspoon baking soda
½	teaspoon salt
1	teaspoon ground allspice
½	teaspoon ground nutmeg
3	eggs
1	cup vegetable oil
1	teaspoon vanilla extract
4	cups peeled, diced apples (3 to 4 medium apples)
1	cup raisins
1	cup chopped walnuts
	Powdered sugar, for dusting

A kettle of lima beans bubbled on the stove while I deepened my postholes. Babe came sliding in on the skis. Something very special this time, a fancy chocolate cake. Sister Florence had sent Babe's wife money to bake me a birthday cake.

—*One Man's Wilderness*, SAM KEITH FROM THE JOURNALS AND PHOTOGRAPHS OF RICHARD PROENNEKE

Apple Cranberry Cardamom Crisp

Baked Alaska ～ SARAH EPPENBACH

5 cups peeled, cored, and sliced tart apples (about 5 medium apples)

1 cup cranberries

½ cup sugar

2 tablespoons lemon juice

½ teaspoon ground cardamom

Streusel Topping

⅔ cup all-purpose flour

⅔ cup firmly packed brown sugar

⅓ cup butter

⅓ cup rolled oats

⅓ cup coarsely chopped walnuts or pecans

The sweet-tart combination of apples and cranberries shows up in many North Country desserts. In this example, cardamom, the favorite Scandinavian baking spice, lends an exotic touch to a satisfying fall crisp.

● Preheat the oven to 375°F. Grease an 8-inch square baking pan.

● Toss together the apple slices, cranberries, sugar, lemon juice, and cardamom and place in the prepared pan.

● For the streusel topping, mix the flour and brown sugar and cut in the butter with a pastry blender or two knives (or use a food processor). Add the oats and nuts, and spread the streusel evenly over the fruit mixture. Bake for 1 hour, or until the streusel browns and the fruit juices bubble around the edges of the pan.

MAKES 8 SERVINGS.

Blueberry Raspberry Cobbler

Baked Alaska ❧ SARAH EPPENBACH

For those who love baking, the glory of Alaska's summers lies in the variety of wild berries rewarding those with nimble fingers and a two-pound coffee can. The combination of blueberries and raspberries produces a beautifully colored cobbler with an intense berry flavor. If you like lots of unadulterated berry juice beneath your biscuit topping, leave out the cornstarch, which thickens the juice very slightly.

- For the biscuit topping, combine the flour, sugar, baking powder, and salt. Cut in the shortening until the mixture resembles coarse meal, then add the milk and mix gently with a fork. Gather the dough into a rough ball and knead a couple of turns to smooth. Chill until ready to roll out.
- Preheat the oven to 400°F.
- Combine the blueberries, raspberries, sugar, and optional cornstarch in an 8-inch square pan, deep-dish pan, or casserole. Place in the oven until the fruit bubbles around the edges of the pan.
- While the fruit heats, pat or roll the biscuit dough to a thickness of ⅜ inch. Cut into rounds or squares and arrange them on top of the hot berries. Sprinkle generously with sugar and return the cobbler to the oven and bake until golden, about 15 minutes. Serve warm, with heavy cream or vanilla ice cream.

MAKES 6 SERVINGS.

Biscuit Topping

- 2 cups all-purpose flour
- 2 tablespoons sugar, plus more to sprinkle on top
- 2 teaspoons baking powder
- 1 teaspoon salt
- 6 tablespoons vegetable shortening (or 3 tablespoons shortening plus 3 tablespoons butter, for additional flavor)
- ¾ cup milk

Filling

- 4 cups blueberries
- 2 cups raspberries
- ½ cup sugar
- 1 tablespoon cornstarch (optional)

Heavy cream or vanilla ice cream, for serving

Blueberry Pie

Discovering Wild Plants ~ JANICE J. SCHOFIELD,
Recipe contributed by Ree Nancarrow, McKinley Park

½ to ⅔ cup sugar
(depending on your
taste and the sweet-
ness of the berries)
1 cup cold water
3 tablespoons
cornstarch
4 cups blueberries
(divided)
1 tablespoon butter
1 prebaked 9-inch
pie shell

• Cook sugar, water, cornstarch, and ½ cup blueberries until thick. Stir in butter, then cool slightly. Put 3½ cups blueberries in the cooled prebaked pie shell. Pour cooked mixture over the top of the berries. Cool until set.

MAKES 6 SERVINGS.

▶ NATIVE WOMEN IN KUSPUKS
CARRYING PAILS OF BERRIES.

Salmonberry Cream Pie

Alaska Wild Berry Guide and Cookbook ◦◦

• Crush 2 cups berries and force through sieve. Add enough water to make 1½ cups. Mix together sugar, cornstarch, and salt and add to berries. Cook, stirring constantly, for 5 minutes or until the mixture is well thickened. Allow to cool. Place remaining 4 cups of berries in pie shell, then pour on cooked mixture. Chill for several hours. Serve with whipped cream and garnish with a few perfect, whole salmonberries.

MAKES 8 SERVINGS.

6   cups salmonberries
Water
⅔   cup sugar
3   tablespoons
     cornstarch
Dash of salt
Whipped cream
Baked 10-inch pie shell

What a man never has, he never misses.

I learned something from the big game animals. Their food is pretty much the same from day to day. I don't vary my fare too much either, and I've never felt better in my life. I don't confuse my digestive system. I just season simple food with hunger. Food is fuel, and the best fuel I have found is oatmeal and all the stuff you can mix with it, like raisins and honey and brown sugar; meat and gravy and sourdough biscuits to sop up the juices with; a kettle of beans you can dip into every day; rice or spuds with fish, and some fresh greens now and then.

—*One Man's Wilderness*, SAM KEITH FROM THE JOURNALS
AND PHOTOGRAPHS OF RICHARD PROENNEKE

Winter Blueberry-Cranberry Pie

The Riversong Lodge Cookbook ❧ KIRSTEN DIXON

2 cups whole frozen
blueberries, thawed
and drained

2 cups whole frozen
cranberries, thawed
and drained

1 cup sugar

3 tablespoons tapioca

Pinch of salt

Pastry for a 9-inch
double-crust mealy
pie shell

2 tablespoons unsalted
butter

Pastry

2 cups all-purpose flour

1 teaspoon salt

1 cup cold
unsalted butter

½ cup ice water

This pie has cranberries added, which give it an unusually rich flavor. I always thicken pies with tapioca rather than cornstarch because tapioca thickens without making the fruit cloudy.

● Preheat the oven to 400°F. Place the blueberries and cranberries in a large bowl. Combine the sugar, tapioca, and salt, and stir into the mixed berries.

● For the pastry, mix the flour and salt together and place on a countertop. Cut the butter into 1-inch pieces. Rub the butter and flour between your fingertips until the mixture is the desired texture (pea-sized for a flaky crust, cornmeal texture for a mealy crust). Add the cold water, a tablespoon at a time, until the dough is just moist enough to form a ball. Flatten the dough with the heel of your hand to layer the butter and flour. Refrigerate for 30 minutes before rolling out.

● Roll out half of the pastry and line a 9-inch glass or ceramic pie pan with it. Spread the fruit mixture onto the pastry. Dot with butter. Sprinkle the rim of the pie shell with a little water to moisten the edge.

● Roll out the remaining pastry and place it over the top of the pie. Seal the edges by pinching with your fingertips or crimping with a fork. Cut slashes in the top crust for steam to escape, and decorate with shapes cut out of any leftover dough. Brush the crust lightly with cold water. Place the pie on a foil-lined baking sheet. Bake on the center rack of the oven for 45 to 50 minutes, or until the crust is golden brown.

MAKES 6 TO 8 SERVINGS.

Baked Alaska

The Winterlake Lodge Cookbook ∽ KIRSTEN DIXON

This Winterlake-simplified recipe of the classic Alaskan dessert is as good as any labor-intensive version. Baked Alaska, called "omelet surprise" or *omelet á la norvégienne,* was served by Thomas Jefferson at a White House dinner in 1802. It was renamed Baked Alaska at Delmonico's Restaurant in New York City in 1876 in honor of the newly acquired territory of Alaska. This recipe contains the safe version of meringue in which the egg whites are heated before being whipped.

8	½-inch-thick slices of pound cake
1	pint vanilla ice cream
½	cup plus 1 tablespoon sugar
2	egg whites
2	tablespoons water
¼	teaspoon cream of tartar
½	teaspoon vanilla extract
1	pint fresh seasonal berries
1	tablespoon crème de cassis

• Using a 3-inch round cutter, cut 8 circles from the pound cake slices. Place a scoop of ice cream onto one round. Top the scoop of ice cream with an additional round of cake. Press down lightly and, using a knife, smooth away any ice cream that has pressed out the sides. Repeat with the remaining rounds of cake. Place the 4 cakes onto a baking sheet and cover with plastic wrap. Place tray in the freezer for at least 15 minutes to firm the ice cream.

• In a large saucepan, bring about 1 inch of water to a simmer. In a metal bowl that will fit over the saucepan, place ½ cup of the sugar, the egg whites, 2 tablespoons water, and the cream of tartar. Set the bowl over the simmering water and beat with a handheld electric mixer at a low speed, moving the beaters around the bowl constantly, for 3 to 5 minutes, until an instant-read thermometer registers 140°F. Increase the mixer speed to high and continue beating over the heat for a full 3 minutes.

• Remove the bowl from the heat and beat the meringue until cool, about 4 minutes. It will form peaks. Beat in the vanilla. Cover with plastic wrap and put in the refrigerator to chill for at least 15 minutes.

• When ready to assemble the dessert, preheat the broiler. In a small bowl, gently mix the berries, crème de cassis, and the remaining 1 tablespoon sugar and set aside. Remove the cakes from the freezer, and quickly spread them with the meringue, swirling it to make peaks. Place the cakes under the broiler, as close to the broiler flame as possible, just to brown the meringue at the tips, about 1 minute. Serve the cakes immediately, surrounded by some of the berry mixture.

MAKES 4 SERVINGS.

Sourdough Bread Pudding with Yukon Jack Sauce

The Riversong Lodge Cookbook ⌒ KIRSTEN DIXON

Sourdough Bread Pudding

½ cup golden raisins
2 tablespoons dark rum
1 pound day-old sourdough bread (about 8 cups), cut into 1-inch cubes
2 cups milk
2 cups heavy cream
3 eggs, beaten
2 cups granulated sugar
3 tablespoons unsalted butter, melted
2 tablespoons vanilla extract
½ teaspoon ground cinnamon

Yukon Jack Sauce

½ cup unsalted butter
½ cup firmly packed light brown sugar
½ cup granulated sugar
1 egg
3 tablespoons Yukon Jack liqueur

Although Yukon Jack is a Canadian liqueur, we have adopted it as our own. This dessert is very popular at the lodge.

• To make the pudding, soak the raisins in the rum for 20 minutes. Preheat the oven to 325°F. Butter a 9-by-13-by-2-inch baking pan.

• Place the bread cubes in a large bowl. Pour the milk and cream over the bread. Let soak for 5 minutes.

• Whisk the eggs with the sugar, melted butter, vanilla, and cinnamon in a medium bowl. Pour the egg mixture over the bread. Add the raisins and rum and toss to mix. Transfer the mixture to the prepared pan. Bake on the center rack of the oven until the bread pudding is golden brown, about 1 hour.

• To make the sauce, melt the butter, the brown sugar, and the granulated sugar together over low heat, stirring until the sugars are dissolved. Whisk the egg in a small bowl. Gradually whisk in some of the melted butter-sugar mixture, then return all to the saucepan. Whisk until the sauce is smooth, without boiling. Whisk in the liqueur. Spoon the warm bread pudding onto dessert plates. Spoon the sauce over the top.

MAKES 8 TO 12 SERVINGS.

Chocolate Bread Pudding

The Riversong Lodge Cookbook ⤳ KIRSTEN DIXON

This pudding is probably my favorite dessert. Vanilla ice cream is a perfect accompaniment.

• Melt the butter in a large, heavy skillet over medium heat. Add the bread cubes and stir until golden brown, about 3 minutes. Transfer the bread cubes to a large bowl; cool slightly. Combine the cream and milk in a heavy, medium saucepan. Bring just to a boil. Remove from heat and add the chocolate. Stir until melted.

• Whisk the egg yolks, brown sugar, vanilla, cinnamon, and salt together in another large bowl. Gradually whisk in the warm chocolate mixture. Pour the mixture over the bread. Top with a small plate to keep the bread submerged in the custard. Let the mixture stand until the bread has absorbed almost all the custard, about 1 hour.

• Preheat the oven to 325°F. Grease a 9-by-9-by-2-inch baking pan.

• Pour the bread mixture into the baking pan. Cover the baking pan with foil. Make several small holes in the foil to allow steam to escape. Set the baking pan in a large roasting pan. Add enough hot water to the roasting pan to come 1 inch up the sides of the baking pan. Bake until the custard is set, about 45 minutes. Cool at least 30 minutes on a rack. Serve warm.

MAKES 8 SERVINGS.

¼ cup unsalted butter
1 pound day-old sour-dough bread, cut into 1-inch cubes (about 8 cups)
2 cups heavy cream
1 cup milk
6 ounces bittersweet chocolate, chopped
8 egg yolks
⅔ cup firmly packed light brown sugar
1 teaspoon vanilla extract
1 teaspoon cinnamon
Pinch of salt

Resident and garden, First Avenue, Fairbanks.

Salads

Green Cabbage Salad

The Riversong Lodge Cookbook ⟶ KIRSTEN DIXON

I love the flavors of cabbage, blue cheese, apples, raisins, and onions all mixed together. This salad is like a cole slaw. We serve it primarily in the winter, accompanied by pureed root vegetables or mashed potatoes, slices of honey-basted ham, and fresh biscuits.

• Finely shred the cabbage into a large bowl. Toss lightly with the remaining ingredients and serve slightly chilled.

MAKES 4 TO 6 SERVINGS.

1 large head green cabbage
1 cup fresh mayonnaise
½ cup crumbled blue cheese
Half a red onion, diced
¼ cup golden raisins
½ cup shredded Parmesan cheese
1 large tart green apple (such as Granny Smith), peeled, sliced, and diced

Salmon Potato Salad

Life's a Fish and Then You Fry ~ RANDY BAYLISS

• Slice red potatoes, boil them until crunchy, and cool them. Add chopped celery, radishes, and green and red onions. Mix in equal volumes of mayonnaise and plain yogurt. Also add flaked smoked salmon. Spice with mustard and dill. Garnish with capers, chopped egg, and so forth. Lemon juice or vinegar will add some zing.

Salmon Pasta Salad

Life's a Fish and Then You Fry ~ RANDY BAYLISS

• Mix dill, chopped shallots, mayonnaise and yogurt, and flaked smoked salmon with cooked and chilled pasta shells. Grated cheese optional.

The milder weather brought other benefits. Palatable herbs sent up their first tender shoots, and under Steller's direction the men dug medicinal plants from the tundra. . . . Now Waxell realized his mistake in not listening earlier to Steller, whom he acknowledged to be a "great botanist and anatomist, well-versed in natural science."

—*Where the Sea Breaks Its Back,* COREY FORD

Live off Our Land Wild Salad and Wild Salad Dressing

Cooking Alaskan ᴄ⤳

Recipe adapted from the *Haines Homemakers' Cookbook*

• Trim, wash, and cut all ingredients into bite-sized pieces. Toss lightly. At serving time, toss again with the following Wild Salad Dressing.

• Mix all but bread cubes together well. Toss with salad greens. Add the bread cubes and toss lightly again.

MAKES 6 SERVINGS.

10 dandelion plants, with blossoms

10 lamb's-quarters leaves

10 leaves of strawberry spinach or plantain (goose tongue)

1 head fresh lettuce, in season, or leaf lettuce

Mustard leaves

Watercress, if available

Wild Salad Dressing

1 cup fresh or canned lemon juice

½ cup salad oil

¼ teaspoon pepper

¼ teaspoon salt

1 small onion or 3 green onions with tops, chopped fine

Juice and pieces from a crushed tomato

Cubed dry whole-wheat bread

Green Lentil Salad with Salmon and Mustard Cream

Salmon ∽ CYNTHIA NIMS
(Northwest Homegrown Cookbook Series)

1½ cups green lentils
1 thick slice onion pierced with 2 whole cloves
1 bay leaf
4 teaspoons thyme leaves
1 clove garlic, minced
3 cups water, more if needed
3 tablespoons red wine vinegar
1 tablespoon minced shallot or onion
1 tablespoon plus 2 teaspoons Dijon mustard
Salt and freshly ground white or black pepper
⅓ cup plus 1 tablespoon olive oil
1 pound salmon fillet, skin and pin bones removed, cut into ½-inch cubes
⅓ cup heavy cream

Raise your hand if you know that Washington state produces more lentils than any other of the United States. It is mighty surprising the number of foods for which the Northwest is a top producer. With Idaho close behind, the two states produce nearly all the lentils grown in the country. I particularly love small, green lentils for this recipe. They have a wonderful, distinct nutty flavor and hold their shape well through cooking. This type is commonly known as *de Puy* lentils in France, though the lentil is grown in the Northwest as well. Regular brown lentils may be used, but take care not to overcook them or they will begin to fall apart.

• Pick over the lentils to remove any stones or other debris. Put the lentils in a medium saucepan with the onion slice, bay leaf, 2 teaspoons of the thyme leaves, the garlic, and water. Bring just to a boil over medium-high heat, then lower the heat to medium-low and simmer, uncovered, until the lentils are tender, 20 to 30 minutes, adding more hot water if needed so the lentils remain just covered.

▶ ALASKA SALMON HUNG UP TO DRY IN SUN, STEVENS VILLAGE.

- Meanwhile, combine the vinegar, shallot, 2 teaspoons of the mustard, and the remaining 2 teaspoons of the thyme leaves in a large bowl with a good pinch of salt. Whisk to mix and set aside for a few minutes to allow the salt to dissolve. Whisk in ⅓ cup of the olive oil, then season the dressing to taste with pepper.

- When the lentils are cooked, drain them well, discarding the onion, cloves, and bay leaf. Add the warm lentils to the vinaigrette and stir gently to evenly mix without breaking up the lentils. Taste the lentils for seasoning and set aside, covered.

- Preheat the broiler. Line a baking sheet with foil.

- Put the cubed salmon in a medium bowl and drizzle the remaining 1 tablespoon olive oil over. Season with a pinch each of salt and pepper and toss gently to evenly coat the salmon cubes. Put the salmon cubes on the baking sheet, spreading them out for even cooking. Broil the salmon about 4 inches from the heat until just a touch of translucence remains in the center of the thickest part, 3 to 5 minutes. While the salmon is cooking, whip the cream to form medium peaks, then whisk in the remaining 1 tablespoon of the mustard.

- To serve, add the salmon cubes to the lentil salad and toss gently to mix. Spoon the salad on individual plates, top with a dollop of the mustard cream, and serve right away.

MAKES 4 SERVINGS.

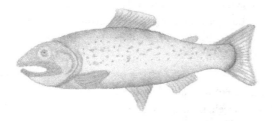

Sesame Steak Salad with Soy-Glazed Oyster Mushrooms

Wild Mushrooms ～ CYNTHIA NIMS
(Northwest Homegrown Cookbook Series)

3 tablespoons soy sauce

3 tablespoons vegetable oil

2 tablespoons mirin (sweet rice wine)

¾ pound oyster mushrooms, brushed clean and trimmed

1 flank steak (about 1¼ pounds)

1 tablespoon sesame oil

Salt and freshly ground black pepper

1 head romaine lettuce, rinsed, dried, and torn into pieces

1 tablespoon toasted sesame seeds

Vinaigrette

3 tablespoons rice wine vinegar or white wine vinegar

1 green onion, minced

1 clove garlic, minced

⅓ cup vegetable oil

2 teaspoons soy sauce

1 teaspoon sesame oil

Flank steak has long been one of my favorite cuts of beef, which my mother typically cooked up teriyaki-style when I was growing up. Using that memory as a starting point for this recipe, slices of the grilled steak embellish a crisp romaine that's tossed with an Asian-style vinaigrette. Tender oyster mushrooms sautéed with a bronze glaze adorn the salad with style. Other wild mushrooms could be used as well, particularly tender varieties such as chanterelle or hedgehog.

• For the vinaigrette, combine the vinegar, green onion, and garlic in a small bowl. Whisk in the vegetable oil, followed by the soy sauce and sesame oil. Set aside.

• Combine the soy sauce, 2 tablespoons of the vegetable oil, and the mirin in a medium bowl and stir to mix. If some of the mushrooms are large, cut them in half. Add the mushrooms to the soy sauce marinade and toss to evenly coat them. Let sit for 15 minutes, tossing the mushrooms 3 or 4 times.

• Preheat an outdoor grill or the broiler.

• Lightly score the flank steak on both sides in a diamond pattern and rub the steak with the sesame oil, then season with salt and pepper. Grill or broil the steak 3 to 4 minutes per side for medium-rare, about 5 minutes per side for medium, or longer to suit your taste. Transfer the steak to a cutting board and let sit for about 10 minutes, covered loosely with foil to keep warm.

• While the steak is resting, heat the remaining tablespoon of vegetable oil in a wok or large skillet over medium-high heat. When the oil is hot, add the mushrooms with the marinade and stir-fry until tender, any liquid the mushrooms give off has evaporated, and the glaze is lightly browned, 3 to 5 minutes.

• To serve, put the romaine in a large bowl. Rewhisk the vinaigrette to mix, and drizzle it over the lettuce with the sesame seeds. Toss well, then arrange the greens on 4 plates. Cut the flank steak into ¼-inch slices at a slight angle and lay the slices over the greens. Top the steak with the glazed mushrooms and serve right away.

MAKES 4 SERVINGS.

· ·

Alaska Cobb Salad

The Riversong Lodge Cookbook ∽ KIRSTEN DIXON

We're allowed to reinvent classics here in the Far North. Smoked halibut, not traditionally found in a Cobb salad, is available by mail order, and it's worth sending away for. I like to serve this salad with a blue cheese dressing, but oil and vinegar can be good, too. Serve the salad with walnut bread and whipped honey butter.

• In a large bowl, toss the greens. Add the halibut, eggs, bacon, cheese, currants, onion, and tomatoes, tossing lightly. Serve with the salad dressing on the side.

MAKES 6 SERVINGS.

1	medium head iceberg lettuce, finely shredded
2	cups mixed salad greens, such as leaf lettuce, cress, and arugula
1½	pounds smoked halibut, flaked
6	hard-cooked eggs, peeled and coarsely chopped
10	slices bacon, cooked until crisp, crumbled
6	ounces Danish blue cheese, or other blue cheese, crumbled
½	cup dried currants
1	red onion, peeled and sliced into thin rings
2	large tomatoes, cut into wedges
	Salad dressing of your choice

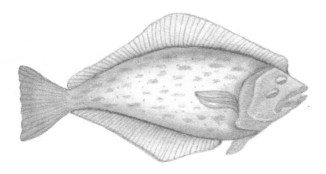

Spring Salad with Mixed Green Dressing

Discovering Wild Plants ∾ JANICE J. SCHOFIELD

1   cup saxifrage leaves
½   cup cleaned cooked
    fiddleheads
½   cup violet leaves
½   cup chickweed
¼   cup dandelion leaves

**Mixed Green
Dressing**
½   cup oil
4   tablespoons vinegar
2   tablespoons
    soy sauce
¼   cup sorrel
¼   cup saxifrage
2   tablespoons
    dandelion leaves

Coarsely chop greens and toss ingredients together well. Top with Mixed Green Dressing.

MAKES 2 TO 3 SERVINGS.

• Mix in blender on high speed.

Warm Mushroom and Spinach Salad

The Winterlake Lodge Cookbook ᕁ KIRSTEN DIXON

This salad is delicious any time of the year, but it seems particularly appropriate in the fall and winter. I think sautéed mushrooms should be nicely salted and peppered, and for this dish I use a fancier salt, such as sea salt from France. If you don't care for bacon or want to dress up the salad a little, try using smoked duck breast instead. For a nice change, add blood oranges and arugula to this salad, if available.

- In a large sauté pan, cook the bacon over medium heat until crisp. Transfer the bacon to paper towels to drain. Pour off the drippings and reserve.
- In a small bowl, combine ¼ cup reserved bacon drippings with the orange juice, shallots, oil, and ¼ cup of the cider vinegar.
- Using a small sharp knife, cut between the membranes of the oranges to release the orange flesh from the skin.
- Place the spinach in a large bowl and dress lightly with the grapeseed oil and the remaining teaspoon of the cider vinegar.
- In a heavy large sauté pan, heat the remaining reserved bacon drippings over medium-high heat. Add the mushrooms and sauté for 5 minutes, or until they are golden brown. Season the mushrooms liberally with salt and pepper to taste.
- To serve, mound ¼ of the dressed spinach on a plate, top it with some of the sautéed mushrooms, pour the warm dressing over them, and decorate with the crisp bacon and orange segments. Repeat for 3 more servings.

MAKES 4 SERVINGS.

ᕁ *Note: Winterlake pepper blend consists of equal parts black peppercorn, white peppercorn, and allspice.*

8	ounces sliced bacon, cut into 1-inch pieces
¾	cup fresh orange juice
3	shallots, peeled and minced
¼	cup olive oil
¼	cup plus 1 teaspoon cider vinegar
4	oranges, peeled, white pith removed
10	ounces baby spinach, washed and dried
1	tablespoon grapeseed oil
12	ounces crimini mushrooms, thinly sliced
	Salt and freshly ground Winterlake pepper blend (see Note)

Ferguson's Fireweed Salad and Mustard Vinaigrette

The Alaska Heritage Seafood Cookbook
ANN CHANDONNET

2 cups fireweed shoots
2 cups lamb's-quarters
1 cup dandelion greens
1 cup willow leaves

Mustard Vinaigrette
1 cup light olive oil
⅓ cup red wine vinegar
or balsamic vinegar
2 tablespoons finely
chopped fresh
parsley
1 teaspoon salt
½ teaspoon Dijon
mustard
¼ teaspoon freshly
ground pepper

"Anything that's green, if you live in Alaska, you value it much more," says Judy Ferguson, who lived on the Tanana River near Fairbanks for 15 summers, on a parcel accessible only by water. After struggling to create appetizing meals so far from sources of fresh produce, Judy says, "I watch my sister in Oklahoma put the tops of onions down the disposal and just cringe!"

Fireweed (*Epilobium angustifolium*) or willow herb is most recognizable in August, when it produces spikes of magenta flowers. In spring, harvest the green and red shoots for a salad rich in vitamin A.

To guarantee mellow taste and maximum crispness, gather the greens early in the season (before the plants bloom) and shortly before you plan to serve them. Fireweed is best when it is 3 to 5 inches tall; it wilts quickly after picking.

● To make the Mustard Vinaigrette, combine the olive oil, vinegar, parsley, salt, mustard, and pepper in a pint jar. Cover tightly and shake well. The vinaigrette will keep for a week in the refrigerator.

● To prepare the greens, trim off any tough stems. Wash well and dry. Tear all the greens into bite-sized pieces, and toss in a serving bowl. Add just enough of the Mustard Vinaigrette to coat the greens, and toss gently. Serve at once.

MAKES 6 SERVINGS.

Kachemak Calamari Salad

The Alaska Heritage Seafood Cookbook ⌒
ANN CHANDONNET

This recipe comes from brewmaster Wade Hampton Miller of Anchorage, who created it for a large gathering, using 8 pounds of squid tubes. (I've modified it here to serve 8.) Wade recommends garlic bread on the side.

• In a large saucepan, combine the water, beer, vinegar, bay leaf, salt, and pepper. Bring to a boil. Add the squid tubes. Return to a boil, and simmer for no more than 60 seconds, until the squid are firm but not overcooked. Drain. Place the squid in a bowl of ice water and stir to firm the flesh. Drain and set aside.

• Slice the squid into ½-inch rings, combine with the lemon juice, and season with salt and pepper to taste. Add the tomatoes, olives, parsley, pimientos, chives, and capers. Toss well. Add the basil, thyme, and oregano, and toss again to distribute the herbs.

• In a food processor, blend the vinegar, garlic, and tarragon. Add the olive oil in a steady stream until blended. Taste, and adjust the seasoning if necessary. Pour over the squid and toss lightly. Cover and marinate, refrigerated, for 1 to 2 hours before serving.

• Serve on a bed of lettuce leaves garnished with alfalfa sprouts.

MAKES 8 SERVINGS.

2 cups water
1 cup pilsner beer
¼ cup vinegar
1 bay leaf
Salt and pepper to taste
2 pounds squid tubes, cleaned
Juice of 2 to 3 lemons
3 large, ripe tomatoes, diced
½ cup sliced black olives
¼ cup chopped parsley
¼ cup minced marinated pimientos
2 tablespoons chopped chives
1 tablespoon drained capers
⅛ teaspoon dried basil
⅛ teaspoon dried thyme
⅛ teaspoon dried oregano
¼ cup balsamic vinegar
3 cloves garlic, minced
1 teaspoon dried tarragon
½ cup extra-virgin olive oil
Red lettuce leaves, washed and dried
1 pint alfalfa sprouts, for garnish

Ginger Soy Seafood Salad

Life's a Fish and Then You Fry ❧ RANDY BAYLISS

2 ounces peanut oil
4 ounces scallops, bite-sized chunks
4 ounces shrimp, peeled
4 ounces halibut chunks
4 ounces thick squid steak, pounded, cut into strips
1 head leaf lettuce, torn into shreds
1 cucumber, partly peeled and sliced
1 bunch green onions, chopped
1 ounce ginger root, grated
1 ounce rice wine vinegar
1 teaspoon soy sauce
1 tomato, sliced

Use the hot wok method for this one. If you have no wok, use a large skillet. I have suggested certain seafood, but feel free to experiment with any other combinations.

• In a hot wok, add the oil and sauté the scallops, shrimp, and halibut for about 5 minutes. Then add the squid, which cooks much faster, and cook for 1 to 2 minutes. Add all the remaining ingredients, except the tomato, and toss the salad in the wok for 1 to 2 minutes more until the lettuce shows the first signs of wilting. Remove from the heat and serve quickly. Add the tomato slices as garnish.

MAKES 4 SERVINGS.

Clam and Bean Salad

Life's a Fish and Then You Fry ❧ RANDY BAYLISS

In Alaska, late winter low tides beckon the foolhardy clam digger, armed with lantern and thermos, to brave snow and darkness for the savory bivalve. I'm not so foolhardy with my thermos—coffee hot as Hell and black as the Moor, with the faint aromas of brandy.

My favorite part of clam cookery is the cooking liquor or broth. I always make extra clam liquor and freeze it. It makes supreme cooking stock or you can quaff it straight up as hot soup. The clams in this recipe make low fat and high fiber less of a penance and more of a pleasure.

• First, dump a gallon bucket of clams into a large kettle and add about a half bottle of dry white wine. Cut the stems off a large bunch of cilantro and add those to the kettle. From a big handful of green onions, cut an inch off both the green ends and the white root ends. Add both of those to the kettle. Cover the kettle and boil the clams until they've opened up. Remove the clams and shell them.

• Slowly decant the clam liquor from the kettle, taking care to leave the greens, sand, and sediment behind. Save ½ cup of the clam liquor for the dressing. I usually drink a ritual cup of clam broth before freezing the rest for later use.

• This recipe calls for 4 cups of cooked white beans, also sold as cannellini beans, popular in Italy. If you use uncooked dry beans, use 2 cups or 1 pound. For cooking dried beans, remember the bean-cooking hints listed on the right. If you use canned beans, rinse the beans well and discard the canned liquids.

• For the salad, chop the green onions and cilantro left from making the clam liquor. Take a pound of snow peas and cut them each diagonally into thirds. Cut a red and green bell pepper into long slices.

• For the dressing, use a blender or food processor to mix the half cup of clam broth with 2 ounces of rice vinegar and a jigger of Rolls Royce–style mustard. With the blender on, slowly add 12 ounces of olive oil, the greenest in color you can find.

• Mix the clams, beans, snow peas, greens, and peppers and toss with the dressing.

SERVES UP TO 8 PEOPLE.

Bean Cooking Hints

- Soak beans 4 hours, changing the water at least once.
- Do not cook beans in the water you soaked them in.
- Do not add salt during soaking.
- White beans should be cooked from 60 to 90 minutes.
- Simmer beans, do not boil them.
- Olive oil will prevent frothing.
- Add water to keep beans covered during cooking.
- Beans are done when you can mash one with your tongue.

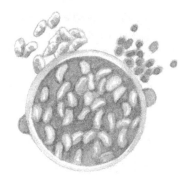

Crab and Sesame Noodle Salad with Sesame Soy Dressing

Crab ∾ CYNTHIA NIMS
(Northwest Homegrown Cookbook Series)

8 ounces somen noodles

2 tablespoons sesame seeds

8 to 12 ounces crabmeat

1 large carrot, cut into julienne strips

1 medium cucumber, halved, peeled, seeded, and thinly sliced

2 tablespoons chopped cilantro

¼ cup sliced green onion tops

Sesame-Soy Dressing

⅓ cup seasoned rice vinegar

¼ cup freshly squeezed lemon juice

¼ cup soy sauce

¼ cup mirin

1 tablespoon finely grated or minced ginger

2 teaspoons Asian sesame oil

In this recipe, tender noodles soak up a flavorful Asian-style vinaigrette, making a tasty base for crabmeat and crisp vegetables. This salad makes a delicious light main course, particularly on a hot summer's day, or serve it alongside a simply grilled piece of fish — salmon would be a particularly good partner.

Somen noodles are thin wheat noodles typically served cold in Japanese cuisine; in the package, they're neatly tied into individual bundles of about 2 ounces each. If you can't find somen noodles, try angel hair pasta instead. Mirin, a sweet Japanese cooking wine made from rice, is available in Asian markets or well-stocked grocery stores alongside soy sauce and other Asian products.

● Bring a large pot of generously salted water to a boil for cooking the noodles.

● While the water is heating, make the dressing. In a small bowl, combine the vinegar, lemon juice, soy sauce, mirin, ginger, and sesame oil and whisk to blend. Set aside.

● When the water comes to a rolling boil, add the noodles and cook just until tender, 1 to 2 minutes. Drain the noodles in a colander and run cold water over them to cool them. Drain again well and put the noodles in a large bowl. Whisk the dressing to mix it and drizzle about three-fourths of it over the noodles, tossing to coat them evenly with the dressing. Cover the bowl and refrigerate for at least 1 hour. (The noodles will soak up the dressing as they sit, giving them plenty of flavor.)

● Lightly toast the sesame seeds in a small skillet over medium heat until lightly colored and nutty smelling, 3 to 5 minutes. Transfer to a small bowl to cool.

● Just before serving, pick over the crabmeat to remove any bits of shell or cartilage, and set aside some larger pieces for garnishing the salad. Add the rest of the crab to the noodles along with the carrot, cucumber, cilantro, and sesame seeds. Toss to mix evenly, and arrange the noodle salad on individual chilled plates.

Scatter the sliced green onion over the salad, drizzle with the remaining dressing, and top with the reserved crabmeat. Serve right away.

▼ BILL RITTER PUTTING CRABS INTO COOKING VAT, HOMER.

MAKES 4 TO 6 SERVINGS.

King crab being offloaded in Kodiak.

Silky Fennel Soup with Alaskan King Crab

A Cache of Recipes ᴖ LAURA COLE

Fennel is often compared to anise, but it has a far sweeter, more delicate flavor. When shopping for fresh fennel, look for bulbs with the greens still attached. The greens will show age much sooner than the bulb. The bulb itself should be heavy and firm. Do not worry if it has some slight signs of browning.

• Trim the fennel down to the bulbs, reserving 8 fronds. Halve the bulbs lengthwise, core, and slice thinly. Set aside.

• In a large, heavy-bottomed stockpot, heat the oil over medium-high heat. Add the onion and sauté until golden. Add the fennel and potatoes. Turn to coat completely with oil. Sauté for 5 minutes. Deglaze the pan with the Pernod. Add the chicken stock and bring to a boil. Reduce the heat and simmer for 25 minutes. When the potatoes and fennel are very tender, puree the soup. Season with salt and pepper. Taste and adjust the seasonings.

• Carefully pick over the crab to remove any shell fragments. Divide the crab among the serving bowls. Ladle the soup on top of the crab. Serve garnished with the reserved fennel fronds.

5 fennel bulbs (about 5 pounds)
2½ tablespoons olive oil
1 yellow onion, diced
1 pound Yukon Gold potatoes, peeled and diced
1 tablespoon Pernod (anise-flavored liqueur)
8 cups rich chicken stock
1 teaspoon kosher salt
1 teaspoon freshly ground pepper
1 pound Alaskan king crabmeat

MAKES 12 CUPS OR 8 SERVINGS.

Nelson Clam Chowder

Lowbush Moose ~ GORDON NELSON

24 small steamer clams
   or 2 8-ounce cans of
   chopped clams
2 cups juice from
   steaming the clams
   or juice from the
   canned clams and
   enough water to
   make 2 cups
2 onions, chopped
4 tablespoons butter
   diced in ¼-inch cubes
2 slices of bacon, cut in
   ⅛-inch pieces
2 carrots, peeled and
   sliced thin
1 teaspoon salt
Black pepper to taste
1 tablespoon soy sauce
1 13-ounce can
   evaporated milk or
   1½ cups fresh milk

My recipe for clam chowder is world famous. Really! One man who has had it is in Cambodia and the other is in Africa. Europe, however, may have to hear of it from this document along with you.

The type of clam used in chowder is not critical. I've found that fresh or canned calms work almost equally well, so you can use whatever is available. I'm giving you the reduced recipe, not the one we usually use, which requires an especially large kettle.

I should mention some of the things that you can use to expand the chowder if you desire. You can always add more clams and milk, but some of the following are good too: 1 4-ounce can mushrooms, lightly sautéed; 1 16-ounce can corn; 1 cup celery chopped fine and sautéed with the onions; 1 cup chopped ham, added to the pot when juice is added; heavy cream instead of milk.

Serve in a tureen if you're going formal or set the pot in the middle of the table if things are informal. Large soup bowls and an endless supply of sourdough bread, and you have a meal to remember.

● Steam open the clams and remove them from the shells, saving the juice and supplementing it with water if necessary. Or open the 2 cans of chopped clams, save the liquid, and supplement with water.

● Sauté the onions in a tablespoon of the butter in your chowder pot, which in my case is my faithful Dutch oven. When the onions are transparent, add the clam juice, potatoes, bacon, carrots, salt, pepper, and soy sauce. Simmer until the carrots are just tender.

● Add the milk, clams, and remaining butter to the pot. Bring the chowder almost to a boil, take it off the heat, and let it set for 5 minutes before serving.

MAKES 4 TO 6 SERVINGS.

Copper River King Salmon Chili

The Alaska Heritage Seafood Cookbook ⌐
ANN CHANDONNET

The dining room at the Reluctant Fisherman Inn in Cordova is famed not only for its pressed copper ceiling—made from copper mined nearby at Kennecott—and its view of the busy small boat harbor, but also for its assertively seasoned king salmon chili. Inn owner (and Cordova's first woman mayor) Margy Johnson told me, "The secret, of course, is the great salmon from the Copper River." Cooks far from a river of kings can use any salmon. For a flavor boost, toast whole cumin seeds instead of using ground cumin. Simply heat the seeds in a dry skillet over low heat until fragrant, about 8 minutes, then grind with a mortar and pestle.

The Reluctant Fisherman dishes up its chili in crispy fried flour tortilla "bowls." Alternatively, warmed flour or corn tortillas may be served on the side.

- Soak the dried beans overnight in the 8 cups water.
- The next day, cook the beans slowly over medium heat until barely tender. Drain the beans and rinse with cold water.
- Heat the olive oil in a skillet. Add the cayenne, cumin, oregano, garlic, green pepper, celery, and onion, and sauté lightly. Add the tomatoes.
- Mix together the 3 cups hot water and the chili powder in a large pot. Add the sautéed tomato mixture and the drained beans. Simmer for 20 minutes.
- Meanwhile, prepare the salmon. Cut the salmon into ½-inch cubes. Bring the 3 quarts of water to a boil. Place the fish cubes in the water and stir gently for 1 minute. Drain in a strainer and rinse gently with cold water.
- Remove the chili mixture from the heat. Fold in the salmon. Garnish each serving with some of the grated cheese.

MAKES 8 TO 10 SERVINGS.

1½ cups dried kidney beans
8 cups water
¼ cup olive oil
½ teaspoon cayenne pepper
1 teaspoon ground cumin
1 teaspoon dried oregano
2 tablespoons chopped garlic
½ cup diced green pepper
1 cup diced celery
1 cup diced white onion
4 cups canned, diced tomatoes packed in puree
3 cups hot water
2 tablespoons chili powder, or to taste
2 pounds Copper River king salmon, skinned and boned
3 quarts water
2 cups grated cheddar cheese

Tart Fish Soup

Life's a Fish and Then You Fry ~ RANDY BAYLISS

6   stalks lemon grass
2   red onions
12 thin slices ginger
1   ounce peanut oil
1   quart fish stock
Chopped peppers or
    paste (to taste)
1   pound prawns, peeled
    with tails left on
2   pounds whitefish (cod,
    rockfish) in chunks
1   cup rice vinegar
1   ounce honey
Sprigs of mint
    and cilantro

Thai cooking blends East Indian with Chinese cooking styles and spices. Hot and sour seafood recipes highlight shrimp, squid, and shellfish.

● Peel and cut the tough parts from the lemon grass. With the flat blade of a large knife, lightly crush the lemon grass. Either grate the onions or puree them in a food processor. Then add the lemon grass, onions, and ginger to the oil in a wok or large skillet and sauté for 5 minutes.

● Add the fish stock and peppers and bring to a simmer. Add the shrimp and fish and simmer for 10 minutes. Just before serving, add the vinegar and honey. Garnish with mint and cilantro.

MAKES 6 SERVINGS.

Botvinyua, a Cold Salmon Soup

Life's a Fish and Then You Fry ~ RANDY BAYLISS

A taste of Russian America.

● Poach about 2 pounds of salmon, chill, and cut into chunks. Clean carefully, trim and puree a pound of fresh spinach leaves. Do likewise with ½ pound sorrel. If you can't get sorrel (which grows wild as sourdock), substitute more spinach and the juice of a lemon. In a large serving bowl, mix the spinach and sourdock together and add a glug or two of dry white wine and the juice of 1 lemon. Peel a cucumber and cut it into strips. Chop a bunch of green onions into 2-inch lengths.

●Add the chilled salmon chunks, cukes, and onions to the spinach-sorrel puree. Garnish with sprigs of dill and place dishes of sour cream and horseradish nearby.

MAKES 6 SERVINGS.

Snapper Stew

Life's a Fish and Then You Fry ⌒ RANDY BAYLISS

Hemingway's deep-sea fishing centered on his boat, the *Pilar*. The boat's master and cook, Gregorio Fuentes, became well-known for his Snapper Stew, highly acclaimed by Hemingway's many famous fishing guests. This calls for one red snapper, whole, without guts, but you can substitute rockfish or bass.

Hemingway's cooking tastes may have matured from bacon grease to olive oil, but he always relished "good, fresh fish." In his later years, his health failed him. A careful diet that included grilled fish helped him control the weight and blood-pressure problems.

• An hour before beginning to cook, take a red snapper and score it several times, cutting diagonally to the backbone. Rub salt into the cuts.

• Select a pan large enough to hold the snapper, head and tail. In it, first make the sauce. Sauté the onion, pepper, and garlic—use plenty of garlic—in olive oil, until the onion turns slightly soft. Add a can of tomato puree, a bay leaf, and oregano. Let this simmer for half an hour. Then add the rest of the ingredients. Simmer for a few minutes more.

• Scrape the salt off the snapper, rinse it slightly, and place it into the simmering sauce. Cook slowly until the snapper turns white and the flesh firms up. Serve, with sauce, over white rice.

MAKES 6 OR MORE SERVINGS.

1 red snapper

Sauce
1 Bermuda onion, chopped
1 red bell pepper, chopped
6 cloves garlic, more if you can take it
Olive oil
1 8-ounce can tomato puree
1 bay leaf
1 tablespoon dried Mexican oregano
1 4-ounce can green olives with pimentos, chopped
½ glass of sherry (you know what to do with the other half)
1 ounce capers
1 ounce raisins

Spring Pea Soup with Crab Mousse

Crab ⌒ CYNTHIA NIMS
(Northwest Homegrown Cookbook Series)

This vibrant green pea soup is distinctly accented with a delicate crab mousse that is subtly flavored with fresh mint. If you're using shell peas, the general rule of thumb is that 1 pound in the pod will produce 1 cup shelled peas, so you'll need 4 pounds of in-shell peas.

2 tablespoons unsalted butter

1 cup chopped onion

4 cups freshly shelled English peas, or frozen petite peas (about 1 pound)

4 cups vegetable stock or chicken stock, preferably unsalted

½ cup whipping cream or half-and-half

2 teaspoons minced mint

4 mint leaves, for garnish

Crab Mousse

5 ounces crabmeat

1 whole egg

1 egg white

2 tablespoons whipping cream

1½ teaspoons minced mint

Salt and freshly ground white pepper

If using frozen peas, be sure to look for the "petite" variety, which tends to be more tender and flavorful than regular frozen peas.

● For the mousse, pick over the crabmeat to remove any bits of shell or cartilage, and squeeze the meat gently in your fist to remove excess water. Put the crab in a food processor and pulse a few times to chop it up a bit, and then add the whole egg and egg white and pulse to form a smooth puree, scraping down the sides a few times to ensure that the ingredients are well mixed. Add the cream and pulse to mix. Transfer the puree to a small bowl and stir in the mint with a pinch of salt and pepper. Refrigerate the mixture for about 1 hour.

● Preheat the oven to 350°F. Lightly butter four ¼-cup ramekins or other small ovenproof dishes (you can use larger ramekins, though the mousse will be shallower and will need a bit less cooking time). Spoon the crab mousse mixture into the ramekins and set them in a baking dish. Add boiling water to the baking dish to come about halfway up the sides of the ramekins. Bake the mousse until it is lightly browned on top, pulls away from the sides of the ramekins, and is firm to touch, 20 to 25 minutes.

● While the mousse is baking, prepare the soup. Heat the butter in a medium saucepan over medium heat. Add the onion and cook, stirring until tender and aromatic, 3 to 5 minutes. Stir in the peas, and then add the stock. Bring the liquid just to a boil, reduce the heat to medium-low, and simmer for 10 minutes.

● Puree the soup with an immersion blender or in batches in a food processor or blender. Pass the soup through a sieve, pressing on the solids with a rubber spatula to remove as much of the liquid and puree as possible, leaving only the tough skins. Scrape the puree clinging to the bottom of the sieve into the soup. Return the soup to the saucepan, stir in the cream and mint, and season the soup with salt and pepper. Gently reheat the soup over medium heat.

● When the mousse is cooked through, carefully lift the ramekins from the baking dish and unmold the mousses upside down onto a plate. Ladle the soup into 4 warmed shallow soup bowls, set a mousse in the center of each bowl, and garnish the mousse with a mint leaf. Serve right away.

MAKES 4 SERVINGS.

Crab and Italian Sausage Cioppino

Crab ⮂ CYNTHIA NIMS
(Northwest Homegrown Cookbook Series)

Bruce Aidells is just the guy to take a San Francisco classic such as cioppino and make it his own without rocking the boat. He's lived in the Bay Area for more than forty years, so he knows a little something about Dungeness crab and the Italian heritage of the region that led to this marriage of crab with tomato sauce, a quintessential seafood stew. But he's also a chef and sausage maker by trade. His embellishment? Hot Italian sausage. You'll be surprised at how well the spicy, rich meat blends with the tomatoes, herbs, and crab. You could use mild sausage instead if you prefer.

Although it's virtually always based on Dungeness crab, cioppino often includes other types of seafood as well. Bruce's original recipe added a few dozen clams or mussels and a couple of pounds of halibut cut into cubes. You may do the same, reducing the number of crabs from three to one, but I have always preferred crab-only renderings of cioppino myself. Sourdough bread is *de rigueur* with the redolent crab stew, as are plenty of napkins.

• Heat the olive oil in a large pot or Dutch oven (about 8 quarts) over medium heat. Add the sausages whole and fry until they are firm and lightly browned, turning them often, about 10 minutes. Set the sausages aside to cool; if there are more than 2 or 3 tablespoons of fat in the pot, spoon out the excess and discard.

• Add the onion and celery and cook until tender and aromatic, about 5 minutes, stirring occasionally. Add the green onion, bell pepper, and garlic and cook for 2 minutes longer.

• Cut the sausages into 1-inch pieces and put them back in the pot along with the tomatoes, stock, clam juice, wine, tomato paste, lemon juice, bay leaves, basil, and thyme. Bring just to a boil over high heat, reduce the heat to medium-low, and simmer for 10 minutes. Add the crab pieces, cover the pot, and cook until the shells are bright red and the flesh is cooked through, 15 to 20 minutes for raw crab (pick into a couple of the thicker sections of body meat to check for doneness), or 10 to 12 minutes for precooked crab.

• Season the cioppino to taste with salt, pepper, and more lemon juice. Remove the bay leaves and discard. Serve at once in

1 tablespoon olive oil

1½ pounds hot or mild Italian sausages

1 cup chopped onion

⅓ cup diced celery

1 cup thinly sliced green onion

½ cup diced green bell pepper

3 tablespoons minced garlic

1 pound fresh Italian plum tomatoes, peeled, seeded, and coarsely chopped, or 2 cups coarsely chopped canned Italian-style tomatoes

2 cups fish stock or chicken stock, preferably homemade

1 cup bottled clam juice

½ cup dry red wine

¼ cup tomato paste

¼ cup freshly squeezed lemon juice, or more to taste

4 bay leaves

(continued ➤*)*

2 teaspoons minced basil, or ½ teaspoon dried

2 teaspoons minced thyme, or ½ teaspoon dried

3 Dungeness crabs (about 2 pounds each), cleaned and portioned, shells lightly cracked if precooked

Salt and freshly ground black pepper

Lemon slices, for garnish

¼ cup chopped flat-leaf (Italian) parsley, for garnish

large, shallow bowls, garnishing each bowl with a slice of lemon and a sprinkling of parsley.

MAKES 6 TO 8 SERVINGS.

Smoked Alaska Salmon Soup

The Winterlake Lodge Cookbook ∾ KIRSTEN DIXON

8 small red potatoes cut into ½-inch pieces

3 cloves garlic, peeled and sliced

1 medium red onion, peeled and cut into eighths

Olive oil

Salt and freshly ground Winterlake pepper blend (page 59)

2 tablespoons finely chopped fresh thyme
(continued ➤)

Vegetable stock paired with fish is a delightful combination for this soup. It offers a delicious harvest flavor.

• Preheat the oven to 350°F. Lightly oil a baking sheet.

• In a medium bowl, toss the potatoes, garlic, and onion lightly with some olive oil. Season the mixture liberally with salt and pepper to taste. Sprinkle the thyme over the mixture. Spread the potato-onion mixture on the baking sheet. Place the baking sheet on a rack in the middle of the oven and bake for 35 to 40 minutes or until the potatoes are fork-tender and brown and the mixture is aromatic. Remove the baking sheet from the oven.

• In a large heavy saucepan, melt the butter over medium heat. Trim the leeks to include the white and pale green parts only. Cut the leeks down their centers and rinse under cool water, fanning them out to remove any dirt. Slice the leeks and add them to the saucepan. Cover and reduce the heat to low. Cook the leeks until they begin to soften, stirring occasionally, about 10 minutes. Don't let them brown. Add the roasted potato mixture to the leeks. Stir in the vegetable stock and bring to a boil. Cover the saucepan, reduce the heat to medium-low, and simmer for about 6 minutes. Add the cream and return the mixture to a simmer. Add the smoked salmon and simmer gently uncovered for about 5 minutes. Add the hot pepper sauce to taste.

MAKES 4 SERVINGS.

4   tablespoons butter
2   large leeks
2   cups vegetable broth
1   cup heavy cream
1   pound hot-smoked (kippered) salmon, flaked
Hot pepper sauce

Wintry Baked Beet and Red Onion Soup

The Winterlake Lodge Cookbook ⌒ KIRSTEN DIXON

I bake beets rather than boil them so they don't lose flavor or color. Sometimes we add baked apple to this recipe or we make beet soup with beef and cabbage added, which is hearty and comforting on cold evenings.

• Preheat the oven to 350°F.

• Wash the beets and dry them. Prick the beets a few times with a fork. Cut the onion in half. Rub the beets and onion lightly with oil. Wrap the beets and onion in aluminum foil and bake in the oven until tender, about 1 hour. Cool the beets and onion to room temperature and peel. Roughly chop the beets and onion. Place them in the bowl of a food processor fitted with a metal blade and pulse several times. Add 1 cup of broth to the mixture and continue to process until the mixture is pureed. Add in the lemon juice. Place the puree mixture in a medium saucepan and stir in the remaining broth. Heat the soup over medium heat and serve hot. Spoon a dollop of sour cream or yogurt on top of the soup as garnish, if desired.

4   large beets
1   medium red onion
Light olive oil
4   cups beef broth
2   tablespoons lemon juice
Sour cream or yogurt, optional

MAKES 4 SERVINGS.

Winter Squash and Halibut Panade

The Winterlake Lodge Cookbook ∽ KIRSTEN DIXON

1 small winter squash
1 tablespoon olive oil
Salt and freshly ground Winterlake pepper blend (page 59)
½ loaf hearty sourdough bread (½ pound)
2 tablespoons butter
1 medium red onion, diced
2 cloves garlic, peeled and minced
8 cups chicken broth
1½ cups grated Gruyère cheese
1 pound halibut

The rich and hearty combination of winter squash, cheese, and halibut becomes a distinctive dish. A *panade* can be thought of as a thick soup fortified with bread or as a soupy casserole. By using less broth, you might call it a bread pudding. You may modify this soup by omitting the halibut so that it's a squash soup—or you may leave out the squash for a fish panade. The dish is best as a main course served with a light salad and perhaps some crusty French bread.

• Preheat the oven to 375°F. Butter a 6-quart ovenproof casserole.

• Cut the squash in half. Scoop out the seeds. Brush the squash with a little oil, and season with salt and pepper to taste. Place the squash skin side up on a baking sheet, cover with aluminum foil, and bake on the bottom oven rack for 1 hour, or just until tender. Set aside to cool. When cool, carefully remove the peel from the squash and cut the flesh into 1-inch cubes.

• While the squash is baking, cut the bread into 1-inch cubes and place the cubes on a baking sheet. Toast the bread on the top rack of the oven for 15 minutes, or until all the cubes are lightly toasted and slightly crunchy.

• In a large sauté pan over medium heat, melt the butter. Reduce the heat slightly and add the onion and garlic. Sauté until tender, about 10 minutes.

• In a medium saucepan, heat the broth over medium heat.

• Cut the halibut into 1-inch cubes.

• In the casserole, spread half of the onion and garlic. Add half of the toasted bread cubes. Then add half of the squash cubes. Add half of the cheese. Add the halibut. Repeat the layering of the onion-garlic mixture, bread cubes, and squash. Top with cheese. Ladle in the broth. Bake, uncovered, for about 40 minutes.

MAKES 4 SERVINGS.

Alaska Fisherman's Stew

Cooking Alaskan ∽
Recipe from *Seafood Moods*

A quick and easy full-meal soup.

• Cut fish into 1-inch chunks. Sauté celery, onion, and garlic in butter in a large, heavy pan until tender. Add tomatoes, tomato sauce, and seasonings. Bring to a simmer, cover, and cook slowly 15 to 20 minutes. Add uncooked spaghetti and boiling water, stir and cover. Cook slowly another 10 minutes or until spaghetti is almost tender. Add fish, cover and cook slowly 7 to 10 minutes or until fish flakes easily when tested with a fork. Serve hot with cheese sprinkled over top.

MAKES 6 SERVINGS.

2	pounds rockfish
1½	cups sliced celery
½	cup chopped onion
1	clove garlic, minced
¼	cup butter
1	large can (29 ounces) tomatoes, undrained
1	can (8 ounces) tomato sauce
2	teaspoons salt
½	teaspoon paprika
½	teaspoon chili powder
¼	teaspoon pepper
1	package (7 ounces) spaghetti
2	cups boiling water
¼	cup grated Parmesan cheese

After breakfast I inspected the red beans for stones, dumped them into a fresh pot of water from the lake, and let them bubble for a spell on the stove. I sliced some onions. What in the world would I do without onions? I read one time that they prevent blood clots. Can't afford a blood clot out here. I threw the slices into the beans by the handful, showered in some chili powder and salt, and stirred in the thick stream of honey. I left the pot to simmer over a slow fire. Come suppertime they should be full of flavor.

—*One Man's Wilderness*, SAM KEITH FROM THE JOURNALS
AND PHOTOGRAPHS OF RICHARD PROENNEKE

Sourdough Soup

The Riversong Lodge Cookbook ∾ KIRSTEN DIXON

½ cup unsalted butter

12 large slices sourdough bread

12 slices Danish white cheese (¼ inch thick), such as Danbo

8 cups homemade or canned beef stock

1 tomato, blanched, peeled, seeded, and chopped

1 clove garlic, peeled and minced

The idea for this soup came from the French version of onion soup. The tomato-garlic garnish can be added to taste.

• Preheat the oven to 350°F. In a large skillet, melt the butter. Fry each slice of bread in the butter on both sides until crisp. Remove the pan from the heat and set aside. Drain the bread on paper towels. Place the bread in a 4-quart casserole or ovenproof soup bowl. Place a slice of cheese on each piece of bread.

• Heat the beef stock to a boil and pour over the bread and cheese. Place the casserole in the oven and bake for 10 to 15 minutes, or until the cheese has melted.

• Meanwhile, add the tomato and garlic to the skillet and sauté until any moisture from the tomatoes is absorbed and the garlic is aromatic. Serve the soup in individual bowls, or family-style, with a dollop of tomato-garlic garnish.

MAKES 4 TO 6 SERVINGS.

Riversong Winter Soup

The Riversong Lodge Cookbook ∾ KIRSTEN DIXON

This soup is Danish in origin. It is a sweet onion, apple, and cream combination that is perfect for a winter's day. Serve it with open-face grilled sausage sandwiches.

• In a large saucepan, melt the butter over medium heat and sauté the onion until golden and softened, about 10 minutes. Add the apples and continue to sauté for an additional 10 minutes. Add the chicken stock, cream, and Calvados. Bring the mixture to a boil, reduce the heat, and simmer for 20 minutes. Season with salt and pepper.

MAKES 4 SERVINGS.

½ cup unsalted butter
1 large yellow onion, peeled, thinly sliced, and separated into rings
4 large tart green apples (such as Granny Smith), peeled, cored, and coarsely chopped
3 cups homemade or canned chicken stock
1 cup heavy cream
2 tablespoons Calvados or applejack
Salt and freshly ground white pepper to taste

In and out of the cabin all day. A kettle of red beans on the fire. Put in bacon rind and bacon chunks and onions and all my favorite seasonings. That's the kind of cooking to do in the wilderness, something that cooks while you do something else and don't have to stand over.

—*One Man's Wilderness*, SAM KEITH FROM THE JOURNALS AND PHOTOGRAPHS OF RICHARD PROENNEKE

Hearty Halibut Chowder

The Riversong Lodge Cookbook 〜 **KIRSTEN DIXON**

3 tablespoons unsalted butter
1 large yellow onion, finely diced
2 large potatoes, scrubbed and diced (about 2 cups)
2 cloves garlic, peeled and minced
6 cups homemade or canned chicken stock
1 can (8 ounces) stewed tomatoes, diced
2 large carrots, peeled and shredded
Salt and freshly ground pepper to taste
1½ cups milk
½ cup heavy cream
2 pounds halibut fillets, cut into 1-inch cubes
½ cup shredded cheddar cheese
Hot red pepper flakes to taste

Besides the salmon, trout, and pike that swim in our river, we have access to other Alaskan seafood, such as halibut. The shredded carrots and cheddar cheese in this chowder make it distinctive.

● Melt the butter in a large skillet. Add the onion and sauté until translucent, about 5 minutes. Add the potatoes and garlic. Cook, stirring well, until the potatoes are crisp-tender, about 7 minutes. Remove from heat.

● Bring the chicken stock to a boil over high heat in a large saucepan. Reduce the heat and add the tomatoes, potato-onion mixture, and the carrots. Stir gently and simmer for 10 minutes. Check the stock for seasoning, adding salt and pepper if desired. Gradually stir in the milk, cream, and the halibut. Simmer, uncovered, for an additional 10 minutes. Reduce the heat to low and stir in the shredded cheese. Sprinkle the chowder lightly with the hot red pepper flakes. Serve immediately.

MAKES 6 TO 8 SERVINGS.

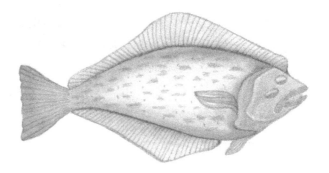

Sweet Potato and Reindeer Sausage Soup

The Riversong Lodge Cookbook ∽ KIRSTEN DIXON

This recipe has great outdoor potential. Sweet potatoes last forever, and this soup is so easy it could readily be prepared on a camp stove.

• Heat the oil in a large stockpot. Add the garlic and onion. Sauté over medium heat until the onion is softened, about 10 minutes. Add the apples and sweet potatoes. Stir in the stock. Cover and simmer until the vegetables are very soft, about 40 minutes.

• Add the cream and stir well. Slice the reindeer sausage and add to the soup. Heat the soup until the sausage is warmed through, about 10 minutes. Stir in the salt, pepper, and hot pepper sauce to taste. Serve immediately.

MAKES 4 TO 6 SERVINGS.

2	tablespoons canola oil
2	cloves garlic, peeled and minced
1	large onion, peeled and diced
2	medium tart green apples (such as Granny Smith), peeled, cored, and coarsely chopped
3	large sweet potatoes or yams, peeled and sliced
1	quart homemade or canned chicken stock
2	cups heavy cream
½	pound Alaska reindeer sausage
	Salt and freshly ground white pepper to taste
	Hot red pepper sauce to taste

I wanted a salad for supper. Fireweed greens make the best, and fireweed is one of the most common plants in this country. Its spikes of reddish pink brighten the land. They start blooming from the bottom and travel up as the season progresses. When the blossoms reach the top, summer is almost gone.

I went down along the creek bed where a dwarf variety grows. None were in bloom yet. I squatted among the stems and slender leaves and picked the tender plant crowns into a bowl. Then I rinsed them in the creek.

Sprinkled with sugar and drizzled with vinegar, those wild greens gave the red beans just the tang needed.

—*One Man's Wilderness*, SAM KEITH FROM THE JOURNALS AND PHOTOGRAPHS OF RICHARD PROENNEKE

Corn-Fish Chowder

The Alaska Heritage Seafood Cookbook ❧
ANN CHANDONNET

8 slices bacon
3 medium onions, diced
3 carrots, diced
4 stalks celery, diced
2 bay leaves
2 teaspoons crumbled dried thyme
4 cups water or low-salt chicken stock
¼ teaspoon freshly ground black pepper
1 green bell pepper, cored, seeded, and sliced
3 potatoes, scrubbed and cut in ¾-inch dice
4 cups fresh corn kernels, cut from 6 to 8 ears
2 cups milk
1 jar (2 ounces) pimientos, drained and diced
8 to 14 ounces cooked seafood
Salt and pepper to taste

The bright colors of yellow, red, and green in this chowder should delight young diners. Teens may even want to try their hand at preparing this recipe themselves.

Leftover grilled corn can be substituted for the fresh corn. Rather than using leftover seafood, raw seafood could be used as well; add it about 5 minutes before the cooked seafood is added.

As the seafood in this satisfying chowder, use one of the following:

8 ounces smoked black cod, smoked halibut, smoked trout, or smoked salmon, cut into ½-inch cubes
12 ounces chopped, cooked clams
8 ounces orange roughy fillets, cut in 1-inch pieces
12 to 14 ounces raw medium shrimp, peeled and deveined

• In a large skillet, fry the bacon until crisp. Remove to paper towels. Pour off all but 2 tablespoons of the bacon fat.

• In the same skillet, sauté the onions, carrots, and celery. When limp and transparent, stir in the bay leaves and thyme.

• In a 5-quart Dutch oven, bring the water or chicken stock to a boil. Stir in the sautéed vegetables. Simmer until the vegetables are tender. Remove the bay leaves.

• Puree the mixture in a blender or food processor until smooth.

• Return the puree to the Dutch oven. Add the black pepper, green bell pepper, potatoes, and corn kernels. Bring to a simmer over medium-high heat. Reduce the heat to low and cook for 8 minutes, or until the potato cubes are nearly tender.

• Add the milk, pimientos, and the cooked seafood, and bring just to serving temperature. Adjust the seasoning with salt and pepper as needed.

MAKES 6 TO 8 SERVINGS.

Halibut Cheek and Wild Rice Soup

The Alaska Heritage Seafood Cookbook ∽
ANN CHANDONNET

During the spring and summer, Kathie Mears of Seward labors on the processing line at Icicle Seafoods. Cheeking halibut heads is an employment benefit that she and her coworkers on the line gleefully anticipate, as halibut cheeks are delicious boneless chunks ranging in size from as small as a sea scallop to as large as one's palm.

One year, Mears says, "I filled my freezer with over 100 pounds of this treat. I've been gradually trying to eat my way to the back of my freezer—trying out new and unconventional recipes." She serves her cheeky soup with Scandinavian rye crackers.

• Heat the oil in a 4-quart saucepan. Add the broccoli, carrots, ginger, and pepper, and sauté for 3 minutes. Gradually add the flour, stirring. The mixture will be sticky.

• Add the water and stir until the flour is thoroughly incorporated. Then stir in the wild rice and halibut. Bring to a boil. Reduce the heat, cover, and simmer for 10 minutes, stirring occasionally. Then add the cream, almonds, and herbes de Provence. Serve at once.

MAKES 4 TO 6 SERVINGS.

∽ *Note: Herbes de Provence is a traditional French blend of dried marjoram, rosemary, sage, thyme, aniseed, and savory, often marketed in a small crock.*

2 tablespoons oil or clarified butter (page 200)
1 cup broccoli florets
1 cup sliced carrots
1 teaspoon finely chopped fresh ginger
1 teaspoon freshly ground black pepper
3 tablespoons flour
1½ cups water
1½ cups cooked wild rice
1 cup raw halibut cheeks or boneless fillets, cut into bite-sized pieces
1¼ cups light cream or half-and-half
½ cup toasted slivered almonds
1 tablespoon herbes de Provence (see Note)

Muktuk Marston holding a salmon, Anchorage.

Smoked Salmon Cardamom Spread

The Riversong Lodge Cookbook ∽ KIRSTEN DIXON

Smoked salmon, sour cream, and cardamom are a flavor blend I discovered one day by accident. We chill champagne in the snow and serve this spread for a special winter appetizer.

• Chop half of the kippered salmon in the bowl of a food processor. Add the sour cream, cardamom, and pepper. Grate the zest of the lemon into the salmon mixture. Squeeze one-half of the lemon's juices into the mixture as well. Process the salmon mixture until it is pureed. Transfer the puree to a large bowl. Coarsely chop the remaining salmon and add it to the puree. Mix well, cover, and refrigerate until serving time. (Other flavorings, such as fresh chopped basil, cayenne pepper, or sun-dried tomatoes, may be substituted for the cardamom.) Serve a dollop of spread on favorite crackers or bread.

MAKES 1½ POUNDS (24 1-OUNCE SERVINGS).

1 pound kippered salmon
¾ cup sour cream
½ teaspoon ground cardamom
Freshly ground pepper to taste
1 lemon

Hot Artichoke and Salmon Dip

Salmon ∾ CYNTHIA NIMS
(Northwest Homegrown Cookbook Series)

1 tablespoon vegetable oil

½ cup minced onion

8 ounces salmon fillet, skin and pin bones removed, finely diced

1 cup prepared mayonnaise

1 cup finely grated Parmesan cheese

1 can (14 ounces) artichoke hearts, drained, rinsed, and diced

Salt and freshly ground white or black pepper

2 tablespoons dried bread crumbs

Crackers and/or baguette slices, for serving

A salmon twist on that timeless classic crab and artichoke dip, this recipe is perfect for a buffet setting, or a cocktail party bite, particularly if you spoon the mixture onto crackers or toasted baguette slices for easy finger food. For some added spice, you could stir in a tablespoon or so of minced jalapeño chile before baking.

• Heat the oil in a medium skillet over medium heat. Add the onion and cook, stirring often, until tender and aromatic, 2 to 3 minutes. Add the salmon and cook, stirring often, until it is just cooked through, 3 to 5 minutes. Transfer the mixture to a medium bowl and set aside to cool.

• Preheat the oven to 400°F. Generously butter a 1-quart baking dish.

• Add the mayonnaise, Parmesan cheese, and artichoke hearts to the bowl with the salmon. Season to taste with salt and pepper and stir well to thoroughly blend. Transfer the mixture to the prepared baking dish and sprinkle the bread crumbs evenly over. Bake until the mixture bubbles around the sides and the bread crumbs are lightly browned, 25 to 30 minutes.

• To serve, set the baking dish on a large plate and surround the dish with crackers and/or baguette slices for scooping or spreading.

MAKES 8 SERVINGS.

Deviled Salmon Skewers

Salmon ∾ CYNTHIA NIMS
(Northwest Homegrown Cookbook Series)

There is some devilish, zesty character in this salmon recipe. It makes for great backyard barbecue fare, offering your friends something to nibble on while the main event is hitting the grill. The same recipe could be used for larger salmon steaks or fillet pieces, to grill or broil and serve as a main course instead.

• Preheat an outdoor grill or the broiler. Soak 12 small (6-inch) bamboo skewers in a bowl of cold water for 30 minutes.

• Cut the salmon fillet into 1-inch cubes. Combine the Worcestershire sauce, vermouth, mustard, and hot pepper sauce in a shallow dish and stir to evenly mix. Add the salmon cubes and stir gently so they are evenly coated with the marinade. Set aside for 15 to 30 minutes to marinate.

• Drain the skewers and thread 3 marinated salmon cubes onto each skewer, skewering 1 to 2 pieces of green onion between the cubes.

• When the grill is hot, lightly rub the grate with oil or lightly oil a foil-lined baking sheet if broiling. Grill or broil the salmon skewers until just a touch of translucence remains in the center, 3 to 5 minutes, turning the skewers once or twice.

• Arrange the skewers on individual plates or on a serving platter and serve right away.

MAKES 4 TO 6 SERVINGS.

1 pound salmon fillet, skin and pin bones removed

¼ cup Worcestershire sauce

2 tablespoons dry vermouth or dry white wine

2 tablespoons Dijon mustard

1 teaspoon hot pepper sauce, or more to taste

6 to 8 green onions

Salmon Roulades

The Riversong Lodge Cookbook ᗢ KIRSTEN DIXON

1 salmon fillet
(1½ pounds)
Salt and freshly ground
white pepper to taste
1 cup fresh cilantro
(coriander) leaves
1 clove garlic, peeled
and minced
4½ tablespoons olive oil
¼ cup shredded
Parmesan cheese
1 cup fresh sourdough
bread crumbs
¼ cup canola oil

We serve this appetizer at the bar with a creamy mustard sauce. But you could serve several roulades along with a Danish cucumber salad as a first course.

● Slice the fillet into 16 thin slices, cutting on the bias. If you are using a huge king salmon fillet, as we often do, cut the slices in half as well. Sprinkle the salmon slices with salt and pepper to taste.

● In a food processor, puree the cilantro, garlic, olive oil, and Parmesan cheese to a paste. Spread the surface of one salmon slice with a thin layer of the cilantro mixture. Roll up tightly and secure with a toothpick, if necessary. Repeat with the remaining salmon slices. Chill until ready to cook.

● Roll the salmon roulades in the bread crumbs to coat lightly. Heat a small amount of oil in a skillet. Sauté the roulades until browned, about 1 minute on each side. Serve on a large platter.

MAKES 16 APPETIZERS, OR 4 FIRST-COURSE SERVINGS.

Babe brought in some fresh groceries
that needed refrigeration. I had dug down a foot into the moss yesterday and found frost. Why not dig a hole and put in a gas-can box, then use my moss-carrying rack with moss for a cover? I think that will do the job. I must put a thermometer in there to find out the temperature. The thermometer in my cooler box under the moss reads forty degrees. And here it is close to eighty degrees today.

—*One Man's Wilderness*, SAM KEITH FROM THE JOURNALS
AND PHOTOGRAPHS OF RICHARD PROENNEKE

Shrimp and Crab Cakes

The Riversong Lodge Cookbook ᴒ KIRSTEN DIXON

Shrimp and crab are available fresh in Alaska all year-round because our coastline is so expansive. I prefer spot shrimp and Dungeness crab for this appetizer dish. Serve the cakes with a favorite dipping sauce—sweet, savory, or spicy.

• In a food processor, puree the shrimp, egg, cream, salt, and pepper. Transfer the mixture to a medium bowl. Add the crabmeat, bread crumbs, onion, mustard, and red pepper sauce. Blend well. Shape the mixture into 2-inch patties, about ¼ inch thick.

• Pour enough canola oil into a skillet to cover the bottom of the pan. Place enough of the cakes into the skillet to fit comfortably without crowding. Sauté the cakes over medium-high heat until one side is crisp and golden, about 7 minutes. Turn the cakes over and sauté on the other side. Drain on paper toweling. Repeat with remaining cakes, and serve warm.

MAKES 36 2-INCH CAKES.

1   pound raw shrimp, peeled and deveined
1   egg
1   cup heavy cream
Salt and freshly ground pepper to taste
1   pound flaked, cooked crabmeat
½   cup fine dry bread crumbs
¼   cup finely minced red onion
1   tablespoon Dijon mustard
¼   teaspoon hot red pepper sauce
½   cup canola oil, for frying

Crabmeat Egg Roll Appetizers

The Winterlake Lodge Cookbook ᴒ KIRSTEN DIXON

Egg rolls are most popular at Winterlake as bar appetizers. Sometimes we spread a little bit of our homemade herbed cheese on the inside of the wrappers, which is delicious. These egg rolls are particularly good made with salmon.

• Bring a 4-quart stockpot filled with water to a boil over high heat. Add the noodles and salt. Turn off the heat and let the noodles soak for about 10 minutes. Drain the noodles and rinse them gently with cold water. Chop the noodles into ½-inch pieces. Place the noodles in a large bowl and season them with salt

2   ounces thin rice stick noodles (*maifun*)
1   teaspoon salt
Salt and freshly ground Winterlake pepper blend (page 59)
1   pound cooked crabmeat
(*continued* ➤)

1 cup finely shredded
  Napa cabbage
1 small carrot, finely
  shredded
2 teaspoons Asian fish
  sauce (*nam pla*)
2 green onions, thinly
  sliced on the bias
16 egg roll wrappers (4½
  by 5½ inches each)
1 large egg, beaten
Peanut oil for frying
½ cup soy sauce
¼ cup mirin (Japanese
  rice wine)
¼ cup rice vinegar
½-inch knob of fresh
  ginger, peeled and
  minced

and pepper to taste. Add the crabmeat, cabbage, carrot, fish sauce, and 1 of the green onions. Stir gently.

• Place an egg roll wrapper onto a dry work surface. Place the wrapper so that one of the shorter edges is closest to you. Place about 2 tablespoons of the crab mixture in the center of the wrapper, spreading the mixture out but leaving the edges of the wrapper dry. Fold the bottom edge of the wrapper over the filling, and then fold the sides of the wrapper into the center. Brush the top edge of the wrapper with some of the beaten egg. Roll the wrapper up, sealing the egg-washed edge to the egg roll. Repeat with the remaining egg roll wrappers and crab mixture.

• Pour about 3 inches of the oil into a heavy saucepan. Heat the oil to 350°F. Working in batches, add the rolls to the oil. Deep-fry the egg rolls until they are golden brown, turning them at least once, about 5 minutes. Drain the egg rolls on paper toweling.

• In a medium bowl, whisk together the remaining green onion, the soy sauce, mirin, rice vinegar, and ginger. Serve the egg rolls with this dipping sauce or with our Dipping Sauce for Shrimp Cakes, below.

MAKES 16 EGG ROLLS AND 1 CUP OF SAUCE.

Dipping Sauce for Shrimp Cakes

The Winterlake Lodge Cookbook ～ KIRSTEN DIXON

5 tablespoons fresh
  lime juice
¼ cup water
2 tablespoons Asian
  fish sauce (*nam pla*)
2 tablespoons sugar
¼ cup minced cucumber
2 teaspoons Asian
  chili-garlic sauce

This sauce is a tasty accompaniment to our shrimp cakes, and it is excellent with our egg rolls as well. When I lived in Thailand as a young girl, every week we went to a Thai restaurant that served shrimp cakes and dipping sauce similar to this. Those flavors still haunt me, and I've tried to replicate the recipe.

• In a medium bowl, whisk the lime juice, water, fish sauce, sugar, cucumber, and chili–garlic sauce to combine.

MAKES ABOUT 1 CUP.

Blue Cheese and Pecan Crackers

The Winterlake Lodge Cookbook ✣ KIRSTEN DIXON

At Winterlake we serve appetizers at the bar every evening at 6:00. These little crackers are favorites. They are delicious topped with a mixture of hot-smoked salmon, sour cream, lemon, and pepper. Another good topping combination is roasted garlic and red peppers.

- Preheat oven to 350°F.
- In a medium bowl, mix the cheese and butter until blended. Using a rubber spatula, mix in the flour, pecans, and salt and pepper to taste. Form the dough into 1-inch balls. Arrange the balls on an ungreased baking sheet. Flatten the balls with a moistened fork. Bake the crackers until they are golden on the bottom and edges, about 35 minutes.

1 cup crumbled blue cheese
½ cup butter
1 cup flour
½ cup chopped lightly toasted pecans
Salt and freshly ground Winterlake pepper blend (page 59)

MAKES ABOUT 24 CRACKERS.

Gruyère Cheese Puffs

The Winterlake Lodge Cookbook ✣ KIRSTEN DIXON

We make these cheese puffs, called *gougères* in French, as appetizers for our guests everyday at Winterlake. Sometimes we make large puffs, slice them, and fill them with dressed salad greens and a sharp cheese for an interesting small sandwich. The dough is *pâte à choux*, which can be sweet or savory. We like our version with lots of pepper. Sometimes I blend bits of hot-smoked salmon into the dough to make an elegant appetizer to accompany champagne. I think the nutmeg and chives are critical to the flavor regardless of what combination you wish to create. Bread flour contains more protein than other flours, which encourages the puffs to rise higher.

- Preheat oven to 400°F. Butter two baking sheets.
- In a heavy-bottomed saucepan, combine the butter, stock, and salt and bring this mixture to a boil. Remove the pan from the heat and add the flour and nutmeg. Using a sturdy wooden spoon,

6 tablespoons butter
1 cup chicken stock
¼ teaspoon salt
1 cup bread flour
¼ teaspoon freshly grated nutmeg
4 eggs
¾ cup Gruyère cheese, grated
(*continued* ➤)

Freshly ground
    Winterlake pepper
    blend (page 59)
1½ tablespoons minced
    fresh chives

stir until the dough is formed and is smooth and shiny. Return the pan to the heat and stir constantly until the mixture comes away from the sides of the pan, about 2 to 3 minutes.

• Transfer the dough to the bowl of a heavy-duty electric mixer fitted with the paddle attachment. (If a mixer is not available, you may leave the mixture in the pan and use the wooden spoon to mix in the eggs.) Cool the mixture for about 1 minute before adding the eggs. On medium speed, add the eggs one at a time, mixing thoroughly after each addition. Add the cheese, pepper to taste, and chives and continue mixing until well incorporated.

• Drop the dough by tablespoons onto the baking sheets, about 2 inches apart. Bake the cheese puffs in the center and lower racks of the oven for about 10 minutes or until they are golden and puffy. Turn the oven down to 350°F and bake another 15 to 20 minutes or until the puffs are hollow in the center.

MAKES 24 SERVINGS.

Barbara's Halibut Dip

The Alaska Heritage Seafood Cookbook ∿
ANN CHANDONNET

2 cups cooked,
    flaked halibut
2 teaspoons sweet-hot
    mustard
½ teaspoon celery seed
½ cup mayonnaise
½ to ¾ cup sour cream
2 tablespoons
    Worcestershire sauce
1 teaspoon lemon juice
2 cloves garlic, finely
    minced
½ teaspoon dried dill
Dash of Tabasco® sauce
Dash of nutmeg

Because Homer is famed for its trophy halibut, the *Homer News* holds an annual Fish, Photos & Fibs contest. In the summer of 1993, Barbary J. Springer won the Fish category. Barbara's rich and creamy dip is an excellent destination for leftover cooked halibut. Other fish, such as leftover grilled or poached salmon or trout or smoked halibut or trout, would be tasty in this great make-ahead party dish, too. Serve this dip with crudités, chips, bagel chips, crackers, or toast points.

• Mix the halibut, mustard, celery seed, mayonnaise, sour cream, Worcestershire sauce, lemon juice, garlic, dill, Tabasco® sauce, and nutmeg, adjusting the seasoning to taste. Chill, covered, for at least 1 hour.

MAKES 6 TO 8 SERVINGS.

Potlatch Plate

The Alaska Heritage Seafood Cookbook ᔆ
ANN CHANDONNET

Rockfish comes into its own when prepared as tempura. This tasty Potlatch Plate of mixed tempura is a popular appetizer at Jeremiah's, a Ketchikan restaurant. Each plate serves several diners. A light dipping sauce sets off the crunchy, battered seafood.

- To make the Tempura Dipping Sauce, combine the stock, soy sauce, sherry, and vinegar, and stir to mix. Set aside.
- Heat 4 inches of oil in a deep-fat fryer or heavy pan to 375°F.
- While the oil is heating, prepare the Tempura Batter: Combine the ice water, egg, and salt in a small bowl; beat well. Add the flour, stirring only until combined. Set the batter in a larger bowl filled with ice water. (Cold batter is a key to a light, feathery coating.)
- Cut the fish diagonally into 2-inch by 1-inch by ½-inch strips. Cut the mushrooms in half. Dip the seafood and vegetables, a few at a time, into the Tempura Batter. Gently add them to the hot oil and deep-fry for 2 to 3 minutes, or until lightly browned. Drain on paper towels. Serve hot with the Tempura Dipping Sauce.

MAKES 3 OR 4 SERVINGS.

ᔆ *Note: Squid fingers are about the size and shape of chunky french fries. Squid rings resemble small onion rings in appearance when cooked.*

Peanut, corn, or safflower oil, for deep-frying
¼ pound rockfish
¼ pound halibut, or squid fingers or rings (see note)
½ pound shrimp
½ pound mushrooms
2 onions, peeled, sliced, and separated into rings

Tempura Dipping Sauce
½ cup chicken stock
2 tablespoons soy sauce
1 tablespoon dry sherry, mirin (rice wine), or fresh orange juice
½ teaspoon vinegar

Tempura Batter
1 cup ice water
1 egg
½ teaspoon salt
¾ cup flour

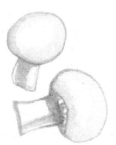

Terrine of Leeks, Scallops, and Sole with Fresh Tomato Sauce

The Alaska Heritage Seafood Cookbook ⌒
ANN CHANDONNET

2 envelopes (2 tablespoons) unflavored gelatin
½ cup water
6 medium leeks, roots and green ends trimmed, washed, and blanched
1 pound sole fillets
½ pound scallops
2 egg whites, at room temperature
1 teaspoon salt
1 teaspoon white pepper
½ teaspoon nutmeg
1½ cups very cold evaporated skim milk
4 ounces morel mushrooms, washed and cut into rings
1 red bell pepper, diced and blanched

Fresh Tomato Sauce
8 large tomatoes
2 tablespoons corn oil
⅓ cup minced chives
1 tablespoon tomato paste

This featherlight terrine was developed by chef Craig McCloud of the Rose Room Deli at Providence Alaska Medical Center in Anchorage. It's a dieter's dream: only 122 calories per serving.

- Preheat the oven to 325°F.
- Sprinkle the gelatin over the water in a small saucepan and let sit until softened, about 5 minutes.
- Line a lightly oiled terrine mold or 9-inch by 5-inch loaf pan with plastic wrap. Chill the terrine for 5 minutes. Halve the leeks lengthwise and separate them into layers. (Remove any grit between layers.)
- Gently heat the gelatin mixture until it is dissolved and smooth. Dip a leek strip in the gelatin and let excess drip off. Lay the strip in the chilled terrine across the width, pressing well into the bottom, with either end hanging over the edge. (The cold terrine solidifies the gelatin so the leeks stay in place.) Repeat with the remaining leeks to line the whole terrine mold.
- Prepare a mousse by whirling the sole, scallops, egg whites, salt, pepper, nutmeg, and evaporated milk in a food processor until fluffy. Fold in the morels and bell pepper.
- Spoon the mousse into a piping bag with a large tip. Pipe the mousse into the terrine mold carefully. Trim excess leek ends to within ½ inch of the filling. Cover the top with parchment paper or the terrine cover. Place the terrine in a pan of hot water and bake in the oven for about 1 hour, or until it reaches an internal temperature of 135°F. (Test with an instant-read food thermometer.) Cool slightly, then chill in a refrigerator.
- Make the Fresh Tomato Sauce while the terrine is chilling. Blanch, peel, and seed the tomatoes, then dice them. Heat the oil in a large frying pan; add the tomatoes, chives, and tomato paste, and sauté, stirring, until the sauce is the desired consistency.
- To serve, slice the chilled terrine and serve it with the hot sauce.

MAKES 6 SERVINGS.

Crab and Avocado Tostadas

Crab ∾ CYNTHIA NIMS
(Northwest Homegrown Cookbook Series)

This variation on the familiar tostada makes great cocktail party fare. The tortilla pieces may be cut and toasted in the morning and then stored in an airtight container after they are fully cooled. Or, for a major shortcut, use good store-bought corn chips in place of the home-toasted tortillas, though the long, slender triangles used here make for a more elegant presentation and are sturdier than many commercial chips. The topping is best made not more than an hour before serving.

- Pick over the crabmeat to remove any bits of shell or cartilage, and put it in a medium bowl. Peel and pit the avocado, cut it into small dice, and add it to the bowl. Drizzle the lime juice over the mixture, and use a fork to lightly mash the avocado while gently blending it with the crab. Add the minced cilantro, jalapeño, and cumin, with salt to taste. Stir gently to mix, and refrigerate until ready to serve. The crab-avocado mixture should be a bit chunky rather than smooth.

- Preheat the oven to 350°F. Lightly brush both sides of each tortilla with some of the oil. Cut each tortilla in half, then cut about ½ inch from the rounded edge opposite the diameter cut. (These trimmings can be discarded or toasted with the rest of the tortillas as a snack for the cook.) Halve the tortilla pieces diagonally to make 2 long, slender triangles, and lay the pieces on 2 baking sheets.

- Toast the tortilla pieces in the oven until crisp and lightly browned, about 10 minutes, switching the baking sheets halfway through. Alternatively, you could toast the triangles on one sheet, half at a time. Let the tortilla pieces cool on a wire rack.

- Just before serving, spoon a generous teaspoon of the crab-avocado mixture onto the broader end of each tortilla chip. Add a tiny dollop of sour cream (if using), and top with a cilantro leaf. Arrange the tostadas on a serving platter, and serve right away.

MAKES 6 TO 8 SERVINGS.

6 ounces crabmeat
1 ripe but firm avocado
3 tablespoons freshly squeezed lime juice
1 tablespoon minced cilantro
½ teaspoon minced jalapeño
Pinch ground cumin
Salt
6 corn tortillas
2 to 3 tablespoons vegetable oil
2 to 3 tablespoons sour cream (optional)
About ¼ cup loosely packed cilantro leaves

Eskimos, king salmon, and kayak, Nushagak.

Double Musky Scampi

The Double Musky Inn Cookbook
BOB AND DEANNA PERSONS

This is one of our quickest and easiest dinners. Total cooking time is about 5 to 7 minutes, not counting the rice. It requires little prep and creates few dirty dishes. We serve this dish with Cajun Rice (page 182).

For the Roasted Pecans: The pecans we buy for the Musky are raw. We roast them in the oven, and the resulting flavor is a great improvement. Just spread them out on a cookie sheet in a thin layer and bake them at 350°F until they darken just a little. Cook them about 15 to 30 minutes, checking frequently. Try some to see if they are done. If they are no longer soft but have a bit of a crunch, they are ready. Remove them from the oven and let them cool.

We use Roasted Pecans in all of our dishes that call for pecans, with the exception of the Pecan Breaded Chicken and the Pecan Pie. The Roasted Pecans would burn in those dishes.

• For the scampi: Heat the olive oil in a large skillet at least 14 inches in diameter; then add the onion, celery, garlic, basil, black pepper, lemon juice, fire oil, and salt. When the onions and celery are almost cooked, add the shrimp. Continue cooking until the shrimp are almost done, then add the sherry, Roasted Pecans, and parsley.

• Finish cooking the shrimp and serve over rice.

MAKES 4 SERVINGS.

½ cup olive oil
4 cups diced white onions
2 cups diced celery
6 tablespoons minced fresh garlic
2 teaspoons basil
2 teaspoons coarse black pepper
¼ cup lemon juice
4 teaspoons Mongolian Fire Oil
½ teaspoon salt
1¼ pounds (31- to 40-count) raw, peeled shrimp, split on underside
¼ cup sherry
1 cup chopped Roasted Pecans
½ cup minced fresh parsley
4 cups Cajun Rice

Nick Jans's Seared Sheefish

The Alaska Heritage Seafood Cookbook ∾
ANN CHANDONNET

1 sheefish, about
5 pounds
¼ cup oil, more if
needed, for frying
1 lime
Freshly ground black
pepper or lemon
to taste

*A*LASKA magazine columnist Nick Jans has fished the fivers of the Western Brooks Range for more than a decade, hooking lunker sheefish. On the trail, Nick and his knowledgeable Iñupiat friend Clarence Wood will divide a 5-pound fish between them and make a meal of it. Nick uses margarine or olive oil on the trail. Home cooks may want to substitute peanut oil, which has a higher scorching point. Lemon juice can be substituted for the lime juice.

• Fillet the sheefish, and cut it into pieces that will fit in a large cast-iron skillet. Place the oil in the skillet and heat until smoking hot. Lay the fish in the skillet with the skin side down. Sear (brown well) over high heat. While the fish is cooking, squeeze juice from the lime over it and sprinkle with black pepper or lemon pepper to taste. Add more oil if necessary to keep the fish from sticking.

• Turn the fillets and sear the other side.

• Reduce the heat and flip the fish over again, cooking it once more on each side.

• Remove the fish from the heat as soon as it flakes and turns opaque within. The heat already in the flesh will finish the cooking.

**MAKES 2 SERVINGS FOR HUNGRY CARIBOU HUNTERS,
8 FOR ORDINARY MORTALS.**

For supper, I cut the trout into small chunks, dipped them into beaten egg, and rolled them in cornmeal. They browned nicely in the bacon fat, and my tender crusted sourdoughs did justice to the first fish fry of the season.

—*One Man's Wilderness*, SAM KEITH FROM THE JOURNALS
AND PHOTOGRAPHS OF RICHARD PROENNEKE

Grilled Trout in Wine Sauce

Cooking Alaskan ◠
RECIPE BY ANN CHANDONNET, ANCHORAGE

- In a small saucepan, combine tomato sauce, wine, butter, lemon juice, green onion, sugar, herbs, salt, and hot pepper sauce. Simmer, uncovered, for 10 to 15 minutes to marry flavors.
- Meanwhile, grill fish over hot coals 10 to 12 minutes. Test for doneness after eight minutes. Turn fish and grill until done. Brush fish with sauce during final five minutes of grilling. Serve fish with warm sauce.

MAKES 6 SERVINGS.

3   pounds pan-dressed trout
1   can (15 ounces) tomato sauce
½   cup dry red wine
½   cup butter or margarine
2   tablespoons lemon juice
2   tablespoons chopped green onion with tops
1   teaspoon sugar
1   teaspoon dried herbs—tarragon, shallots, parsley
½   teaspoon salt
A few drops bottled hot pepper sauce (optional)

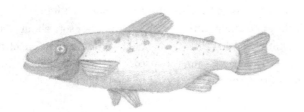

··

Butter Clams Steamed with Aromatics

The Alaska Heritage Seafood Cookbook ◠
ANN CHANDONNET

Butter clams steamed with herbs, olive oil, and white wine is simple, speedy, and sure to please a medley of demanding gourmets. Serve with crusty bread to sop up the juices.

- Heat a large, heavy pot on medium heat without added water. Add the olive oil, garlic, lemon zest, onion, rosemary, lemon juice, and wine.
- When the mixture boils, add the clams. Cover and cook

2   tablespoons olive oil
4   cloves garlic, chopped
Grated zest of ½ lemon
¼   cup minced onion, or 2 teaspoons dried onion flakes

(*continued* ➤)

1 tablespoon chopped
  fresh rosemary
Juice of 1 lemon
1 cup dry white wine
4 pounds small butter
  clams, scrubbed

over high heat for 7 minutes, or until the clams open, shaking the pot every 2 minutes to redistribute the clams. If the pot goes dry, add ¼ cup water. Discard any clams that do not open. Strain the pan juices through a strainer or colander lined with moistened cheesecloth to remove any sand.

• Serve the clams with the cooking juices in soup bowls.

MAKES 4 APPETIZER SERVINGS.

Risotto with Clams

The Alaskan Camp Cook ∾
RECIPE BY EUNICE AND RAY NEVIN, JUNEAU

¼ cup cooking oil
1 onion, chopped fine
1 clove garlic, chopped
  fine
2 cups canned tomatoes
  (clam broth may
  furnish part of this
  quantity)
2 tablespoons chopped
  parsley (optional)
Pinch of basil (optional)
1 cup raw rice
¾ teaspoon salt
2 cups minced clams,
  or equivalent in fresh
  clams in shell

Sauté onions and garlic lightly in oil, add all but the clams, cover tightly and steam until rice is tender but not soft, about 15 to 20 minutes. Add clams, cover, and heat until flavors are blended.

• When fresh clams are used, place well-scrubbed clams on top of rice, cover, and steam until shells open.

MAKES 4 TO 6 SERVINGS.

A handsome grayling all aglitter with silver, *purple, and blue. Seventeen and a quarter inches long, enough for my needs. I watched the grayling feast on what the current brought them. What a sight it would be to put on a wet suit and mask and visit the grayling at their evening banquet down under.*

—*One Man's Wilderness*, SAM KEITH FROM THE JOURNALS
AND PHOTOGRAPHS OF RICHARD PROENNEKE

Linguini con Vongole

Life's a Fish and Then You Fry ~ RANDY BAYLISS

More pasta and seafood on Bellezza's (a well-known seafood restaurant formerly in Juneau) menu included fresh clams in a sauce of cream, white wine, olive oil, and butter, topped with Parmesan cheese, served over linguini. The cream sauce goes like this: to 4 ounces of heavy cream, add 1 ounce of white wine, 1 ounce of olive oil, 1 teaspoon of garlic puree, and a few drops of lemon juice. Notice how the subtlety of spices in a cream sauce compares with the rich tomato-based sauces. Add 4 ounces of chopped steamed clams and the juices. Reduce by simmering for 10 minutes. Toss linguini with soft butter, add the clam sauce, and garnish with grated Parmesan cheese.

MAKES 2 SERVINGS.

Cordova Crab

Cooking Alaskan ~ RECIPE BY PANSY BRAY,
Seaword

4	Dungeness crabs, cooked
2	cups salad oil
1	cup vinegar
2	tablespoons lemon juice
1	tablespoon soy sauce
1	tablespoon chopped parsley
4	cloves garlic, finely crushed
1	large onion sliced

Marinated in the shell.

• Clean the crab. Separate the body and leg sections. Crack legs to allow marinade to flavor the meat. Place crab in a deep bowl.

• Mix other ingredients and pour the marinade over the crabs. Use basting tube to pour the sauce over the crabs for several minutes.

• Cover the bowl and refrigerate. Every half hour for 4 hours, repeat the basting process. Serve cold, as an appetizer or an entrée.

MAKES 6 TO 8 SERVINGS.

Curried Crab Casserole

The Alaska Heritage Seafood Cookbook ⌒
ANN CHANDONNET

1½ pounds broccoli
1 cup grated sharp cheddar cheese
¼ cup butter or margarine
2 tablespoons chopped onion
2 tablespoons flour
¼ tablespoon curry powder or more to taste, up to 1 tablespoon
½ tablespoon salt
1 cup milk
1 tablespoon lemon juice
2 cups crabmeat
⅓ cup dry bread crumbs

Kathy Hunter, a humorist and writing instructor, who formerly lived in Fairbanks and before that hailed from king crab country—Kodiak Island—passed along this entrée. Kathy has built her home-style dish around fresh broccoli harvested from her bountiful garden on Lazy Mountain outside Palmer. Serve with steamed jasmine rice along with mango chutney, slices of peeled kiwi fruit, or fresh pineapple spears on the side.

● Cut broccoli florets from the stalks. Peel the stalks and slice 1 inch thick. Steam the florets and stalks on a rack over simmering water for 3 or 4 minutes, or until just tender but not limp.

● Arrange the broccoli in the bottom of a buttered casserole dish. Sprinkle the grated cheese over the broccoli.

● Preheat the oven to 350°F.

● In a frying pan, melt the butter and sauté the onion for 3 to 4 minutes. Stir in the flour, curry powder, and salt. Cook and stir for 2 minutes to eliminate any floury taste. Gradually stir in the milk. Cook and stir until thick. Add the lemon juice and crabmeat.

● Pour the crab mixture over the broccoli and sprinkle with the bread crumbs. Bake for 30 minutes.

MAKES 6 SERVINGS.

No tent tonight in Thompson Pass. Jane and I have climbed above the bugs. The warmth, too. It's near freezing as I cook dinner. Our kitchen table is a rock scarred with corduroy lines by a retreating glacier.

—*Walking My Dog, Jane,* NED ROZELL

Tequila Lime Scallops

The Alaska Heritage Seafood Cookbook ∾
ANN CHANDONNET

This eclectic recipe was invented by chef Peter Ostrinsky for the Raven's Nest Restaurant in Fairbanks. "We've gotten lots of compliments on it," says Ostrinsky, now a resident of Anchorage. Ostrinski first became acquainted with a restaurant kitchen when he worked as a dishwasher in Scribners, a four-star seafood house in his hometown, Milford, Connecticut. Just 15 then, he was sufficiently intrigued to set his sights on graduating from the Culinary Institute of America. He later worked at another four-star establishment, the Occidental, in Washington, D.C. After three years of electrical construction in Fairbanks, he dived back into cooking, rising to the level of sous-chef at the Raven's Nest.

Serve these scallops with wild rice pilaf and the fresh vegetable of your choice.

● Heat a large sauté pan until medium hot. Add the butter, followed by the scallops. When slightly browned, turn the scallops and add the herbs, garlic, salt, pepper, and tequila. Be careful when adding tequila; it will flame up in the pan, which burns off the alcohol.

● While the sauté is flaming, shake the pan to deglaze it, or loosen the flavorful food solids from the bottom of the pan.

● When the flames subside, pour in the lime juice and allow the mixture to simmer for 2 to 3 minutes. When the scallops are semi-firm, remove them from the pan and keep warm. Continue to simmer the sauce until it reaches a syrupy consistency. Arrange the scallops on 4 warmed plates. Pour the sauce over the scallops and serve.

MAKES 4 SERVINGS.

½ cup Clarified Butter (**page 200**) or extra-virgin olive oil

2 pounds sea scallops

2 tablespoons chopped fresh herbs (a mixture of basil, oregano, thyme, chives, and mint)

2 tablespoons finely chopped garlic

2 teaspoons salt, or to taste

1 teaspoon freshly ground white pepper, or to taste

1½ cups gold tequila, preferably José Cuervo

1½ cups Rose's lime juice or fresh lime juice

Broiled Salmon in Horseradish Ginger Crust

The Riversong Lodge Cookbook ⤳ KIRSTEN DIXON

3 cups fine fresh
   sourdough bread
   crumbs
1 cup unsalted butter
⅓ cup grated fresh
   horseradish
¼ cup grated fresh
   ginger
Salt and freshly ground
   white pepper to taste
8 salmon fillets
   (6 ounces each)

The crust on this fish also works well for chicken and other game birds. We make a soy sauce–sake broth to serve alongside: combine two parts fish stock to one part soy sauce, with sake added to taste, then boil the mixture until reduced by half.

● Preheat the broiler. Grease a baking sheet. Combine the bread crumbs, butter, horseradish, and ginger in a food processor, working it into a smooth paste. Season with salt and pepper to taste. Spread some of the paste on top of each fillet. Place the fillets on a greased baking sheet. Broil the fish at least 2 inches from the heat source until the crust is golden brown, about 10 minutes. Serve hot.

MAKES 8 SERVINGS.

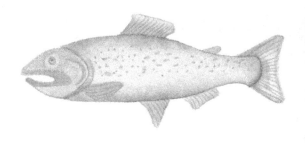

Alaska Salmon Burgers

The Winterlake Lodge Cookbook ❧ KIRSTEN DIXON

Chiffonade" is a word of French origin meaning "crumbled like a rag." It means to finely cut strips of green leafy vegetables or herbs. Lately I've been serving salmon burgers on a slice of rustic toasted bread topped with fresh greens. I have been making these salmon burgers for my lodge guests for twenty years and they are still a popular favorite. Serve each burger topped with Apple Cherry Chutney (page 201) or Cranberry Chutney (page 202).

- Cut the salmon into ¼-inch dice. In a medium bowl, mix the salmon, red onion, and basil until they are well combined, adding salt and pepper to taste.

- Beat the egg white in a small bowl and add it and the hot pepper sauce to the salmon mixture. Form the salmon mixture into four ½-inch-thick patties.

- Heat a 12-inch nonstick sauté pan over medium heat. Lightly brush the pan with a little oil. Cook the patties, carefully turning once, until they are golden brown and cooked through, about 6 to 7 minutes total.

MAKES 4 BURGERS.

Salmon fillet (1 pound), boneless and skinless
½ small red onion, minced
¼ cup basil, cut into chiffonade
Salt and freshly ground Winterlake pepper blend (page 59)
1 egg white
1 tablespoon hot pepper sauce
Light olive oil

Salmon Omelet Pie

The Alaska Heritage Seafood Cookbook ∾
ANN CHANDONNET

2   tablespoons oil
5   potatoes, scrubbed
    and diced
1   small onion, chopped
⅓   pound mushrooms,
    sliced
8   eggs
½   cup milk
2   tablespoons flour
Salt and freshly ground
    pepper to taste
Garlic powder to taste
1½ cups cooked and
    chunked salmon,
    bones removed
1½ cups grated cheddar
    cheese

Hook-M-Up tours in Aniak, on the banks of the Kuskokwim, is a small fishing lodge known to its clients as the "Kuskokwim Hilton." Fish, served every day, is seldom cooked the same way twice, says lodge owner Woody Wooderson. "We've been told that if the fishing ever gets bad, we can always start a restaurant."

One of Woody's favorite dishes is this frittata-like omelet. On the riverbank, Woody wields a 24-inch skillet to cook up 2 dozen eggs at a time—enough to serve 12. His recipe has been trimmed here for home cooks.

For a low-fat variation, boil the potatoes instead of frying, combine them with the other ingredients (using skim milk if you like), and bake instead of fry. Sprinkle low-fat cheese on top, let it melt, and serve.

• Heat the oil in a 12- or -14 inch skillet. Fry the diced potatoes until golden and almost fork-tender, about 5 minutes. Add onion and fry another 2 minutes. Add mushrooms; cover and cook for 1 more minute.

• Meanwhile, in a large bowl whip the eggs, milk, flour, salt, pepper, and garlic powder vigorously until thoroughly mixed.

• Pour the egg mixture over the potato mixture in the skillet. Fold in the salmon. Cover the pan and cook over low heat until the eggs are set.

• Remove from the heat. Sprinkle the cheese on top of the entire omelet, cover, and allow to rest. As soon as the cheese is melted, cut the omelet into wedges and serve.

MAKES 4 TO 5 SERVINGS.

Spinach Pesto with King Salmon

Life's a Fish and Then You Fry ⌒ RANDY BAYLISS

Spinach and salmon make an outstanding match, but only if you use fresh spinach. Save the canned spinach to punish misbehaving children.

• Broil or poach the salmon, about 10 minutes per inch of thickness. Place 1 cup of spinach leaves in a food processor; add the pesto and oil and blend. Serve the salmon on beds of spinach leaves and garnish with spinach pesto.

MAKES 4 SERVINGS.

4	king salmon fillets or steaks, 6 ounces each
4	cups fresh spinach leaves, divided
1	ounce pesto (page 200)
1	ounce olive oil

▼ Native Alaskan girls drying salmon.

Laurie's Grilled Salmon Fillets

The Alaska Heritage Seafood Cookbook
ANN CHANDONNET

- ½ cup butter, melted
- ¾ cup finely chopped onion
- ¼ cup Worcestershire sauce
- ¼ teaspoon garlic powder, or fresh, pressed garlic to taste
- 4 pounds salmon fillets, with skin left on

Summer" and "barbecued salmon" are synonymous for hordes of grill-happy Alaskans. Among these hordes is Laurie Johnson.

For more than six years, Johnson has cooked at Denali Center, a Fairbanks nursing home. Because many of Johnson's charges are Native Americans, she regularly receives donations of fish or game to prepare for the residents. Her grilled salmon is one of their favorites.

"I have a charcoal grill right on the deck outside the kitchen," Johnson says. "I do it year-round, even if it's 40 or 50 below. Of course, when it's cold, the fish *does* take longer to cook!" Vary the seasonings according to your whim.

• Light the coals. In a small bowl, combine the butter, onion, Worcestershire sauce, and garlic powder. When the coals are at the proper state, place the filleted fish on the grill, skin side down, for 10 to 15 minutes. Cover fish with foil or the grill lid. Baste with the butter mixture as the fish cooks. Milky solids will coagulate on the fillets when they are cooked through. To check on cooking, cut into one fillet. If flesh is still raw in center, continue cooking.

MAKES 8 TO 12 SERVINGS.

Praline Halibut

The Alaska Heritage Seafood Cookbook
ANN CHANDONNET

- ½ cup butter, softened
- ½ cup light brown sugar
- ½ cup finely ground pecans

(*continued* ➛)

Legal whiz A. Isabel Lee of Anchorage smacks her lips when talking about this exuberantly buttery entrée, which she first encountered in Florida restaurants. No counting calories here! The dish was originally made with grouper; now that she's settled in Alaska, Lee uses halibut. Serve with individual loaves of sourdough bread, pasta, or small red potatoes—something to soak up the drippings.

- Combine the softened butter, brown sugar, and pecans. Mix well and set aside.

- Sprinkle the fish with the lemon juice, salt, and pepper. Dust lightly with the flour.

- Heat the Clarified Butter over medium-high heat in a sauté pan. When hot, add the fish. Cook until the fish is golden brown on one side, 4 to 6 minutes. Turn, cover, and continue cooking on low heat until the fish is cooked through (about 4 more minutes).

- Remove the fish to a warm serving dish. Pour off the excess clarified butter. Add the pecan butter mixture to the pan. When the butter begins to foam, pour it over the fillets. Sprinkle with parsley. Serve immediately.

MAKES 6 SERVINGS.

3 pounds halibut fillets
Juice of 2 lemons
Salt and white pepper to
    taste
½ cup flour
¼ cup Clarified Butter
    (page 200)
Chopped fresh parsley,
    for garnish

◀ Two men standing next to a 300-pound halibut hanging from block and tackle, Juneau.

Baked Halibut with Tomatoes and Onion

The Winterlake Lodge Cookbook ❧ KIRSTEN DIXON

½ cup light olive oil
½ cup finely chopped fresh Italian parsley
3 garlic cloves, minced
4 halibut steaks (about 2 pounds)
1½ pounds tomatoes, diced
2 large yellow onions, thinly sliced
Salt and freshly ground Winterlake pepper blend (page 59)
1 cup vegetable broth

This dish is easy to prepare and goes well with buttery rice. If you want the broth to be more Mediterranean, replace some of the vegetable broth with some white wine. Also, you can replace the vegetable broth with fish broth if you prefer. If you like food a little spicy, splash a few dashes of hot pepper sauce over the dish right before placing it in the oven.

• Preheat the oven to 350°F.

• In a small bowl, combine the oil, parsley, and garlic.

• Trim the halibut, if necessary, to remove any skin, bones, or fat. Rub the halibut steaks thoroughly with the oil and spice mixture. Place the halibut and any remaining oil and spice mixture into Ziploc-style bags. Seal and place in the refrigerator to marinate for about 1 hour.

• Arrange half of the tomatoes and onions on the bottom of a 9-by-9-by-2-inch baking dish. Add the fish fillets and marinade, then top the fish with a layer of the remaining tomatoes and onions. Season the vegetables liberally with salt and pepper to taste. Pour the vegetable broth over the fish and vegetables. Cover the baking dish and bake for about 20 minutes, or until the fish is tender, the broth is bubbling, and the onions and tomatoes are aromatic.

MAKES 4 SERVINGS.

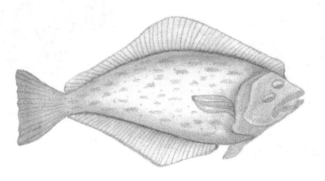

FISH, SHELLFISH

Halibut Supreme

Cooking Alaskan ⌒ RECIPE BY BOB HENNING, ANGOON
Founder of Alaska Northwest Books

A casserole that will serve many . . . or a few, with several extra meals for the freezer.

• Mix the fish chunks with the next 11 ingredients. Place in large, greased baking dish. Cover top with thin slices of sharp cheddar cheese. Bake for 45 minutes at about 350°F. Then add thin slices of green pepper and sliced, stuffed olives to the top and sprinkle all with Parmesan cheese. Bake another half hour.

MAKES AT LEAST 12 SERVINGS.

1½ to 2 pounds boneless halibut chunks
1 29-ounce can whole tomatoes with juice
1 8-ounce can tomato sauce
About 1 pint milk
1 10-ounce can mushroom soup, diluted with 1 can water
1 4-ounce can mushroom pieces and stems
1 4½-ounce can chopped black olives
A handful of dry onion flakes
A handful of parsley flakes
1 4½-ounce can tiny shrimp
Half a dozen stale rolls (sourdough is best), broken into pieces
Salt and pepper to taste
Sharp cheddar cheese
Green pepper rings
Sliced, stuffed olives
Parmesan cheese, grated

The fish wheel is a simple device. Two wire baskets and two paddles, like four spokes on a wheel, radiate from a large wooden axle. River current turns the device, and as it rotates, the baskets scoop fish from the river and deposit them in a collecting box. When placed directly over a place where the salmon pass, each revolution of a basket has a chance of picking up fish.

We set the fish wheel to turning and almost immediately started catching chum salmon. Charlie Evans taught us how to cut the fish for dog food and Jimmie and I quickly learned the technique. We cut and split the fish and kept Dad more than busy hanging them on the drying racks we had built. With practice we were able to process 800 six-to-eight pound salmon a day. By the Fourth of July, we had 5,000 salmon dried or hanging on the drying racks. We smoked some of the choicer fish to eat ourselves.

—*Shadows on the Koyukuk*,
SIDNEY HUNTINGTON WITH JIM REARDEN

Halibut Delmonico

Cooking Alaskan ~ DR. ERNEST GRUENING,
PTA Cookbook, Petersburg

6 halibut fillets
1 onion, sliced
1 pint milk
2 tablespoons butter
   or margarine
2 tablespoons flour
2 tablespoons sherry
1 cup fresh, seedless
   white grapes
Grated cheese
Bread crumbs
Additional butter or
   margarine

Grayling, black cod, and trout are also good fixed this way.
 • Place the fish fillets in a large kettle with the sliced onion
and just enough milk to cover—about 1 pint. Simmer about 8
minutes until fish is tender but not broken. Grease a large, flat
casserole and place the cooked fish in it, reserving the milk.
 • In a small saucepan, over medium heat, mix butter and
flour until bubbly and well blended. Gradually add the milk in
which the fish was cooked to make a cream sauce. Add sherry and
seedless grapes, and pour over fish. Sprinkle generously with
grated cheese and bread crumbs and dot with butter. Bake in a
moderate oven, 350°F, until well heated and crumbs are browned.

MAKES 6 SERVINGS.

Cod Baked with Sun-Dried Tomato-Thyme Butter

The Alaska Heritage Seafood Cookbook ~
ANN CHANDONNET

1 cup flour
1 teaspoon salt
1 teaspoon freshly
   ground black pepper
Pinch of granulated garlic
   or onion powder
   (*continued* ➤)

For years, chef Darin Hudson delighted diners at Simon &
Seafort's Saloon & Grill in Anchorage with his inventive flavorings
for baked and broiled fish.
 • To make the Sun-Dried Tomato-Thyme Butter, dice the
tomatoes in ¼-inch pieces. Whip the butter until smooth. Blend
together the butter, shallots, garlic, thyme, and lemon juice. When
well combined, add the tomatoes and gently fold just until incorporated. Makes 1 cup.
 • Preheat the oven to 400°F.

• Combine the flour with the salt, pepper, and granulated garlic, and place on a plate or in a shallow bowl. In a separate shallow bowl, combing the eggs with the milk.

• Dredge the cod fillets in the seasoned flour, then dip in the egg mixture. Place in a greased baking pan. Spread each fillet with 2 to 3 tablespoons of the Sun-Dried Tomato-Thyme Butter. Bake until the fish is cooked through, 6 to 12 minutes. Garnish each serving with a lemon wedge, a thyme sprig, and a tomato fan.

MAKES 4 SERVINGS.

~ *Note: To make tomato fans, choose tomatoes no larger than 2 inches in diameter. Holding a tomato by the stem end, slice almost through the tomato at ¼- to ⅓-inch intervals, leaving the slices attached at the stem end. Fan out the resulting blades to resemble a fan.*

2 eggs, lightly beaten
1 cup milk
2 pounds cod fillets
4 lemon wedges, for garnish
4 sprigs thyme, for garnish
4 tomato fans (see Note) or tomato wedges, for garnish

Sun-Dried Tomato-Thyme Butter

½ cup sun-dried tomatoes packed in olive oil, drained
1 cup softened butter
1 tablespoon minced shallots
1 teaspoon minced garlic
1½ tablespoons chopped fresh thyme or 1 teaspoon dried thyme
1 tablespoon fresh lemon juice

Burning my fingers, I unwrap the foil.
The grayling's skin sticks to the metal, exposing delicate rows of white flesh. The first taste, buttery and clean, makes me wish we'd caught a few more.

I swirl the flesh on my tongue while looking at the creek in which the fish was spawned. This feeling of communion is why I like to fish, to hunt. We are a part of the country as we eat of it, as it fuels our bodies. We become the fish, the moose, the caribou. The killing is the least pleasant part; it has nothing to do with the excitement I feel when hunting or fishing. Killing is a necessary part of the process, the bad part. As grayling dissolves on the back of our tongues, we experience the good.

—*Walking My Dog, Jane,* NED ROZELL

Smoked Fish

The Alaskan Camp Cook ⌁
RECIPE BY G. S. "BUD" MORTENSEN, PETERSBURG

Only fresh, fat, sea-run fish are ideal for smoking. In order of quality they are: king salmon, steelhead trout, sockeye, chum, coho (silver) salmon.

- First step in preparation is to fillet the fish. Fish under 12 pounds can be smoked "in the side," suspended by the neck end from a wire hook. For larger fish, such as the king salmon, cut the flesh side cross-wise, following the ribs, at 1-inch intervals. Wash well in cold water.
- To 4 gallons of water add 3½ quarts rock salt and 1 pound brown sugar. Stir occasionally until well dissolved. Soak fish 30 minutes in this brine. Lay out on slightly tilted board to drain. Hang fish in the smokehouse by means of wire hooks or heavy white string, not less than 4 feet above fire. Always hang fish with tail end down. This is very important. A baffle of tin about 2 feet above the fire is a good arrangement to divert direct heat and ash from fish.
- Green alder is best, and a slow, continuous smoke fire for 40 hours or less, depending upon size of fish and degree of heat. For the first 10 to 12 hours keep the smokehouse door partly open to assure "setting up" of fish and prevent falling. Scrape any excess moss from alder before using.
- For kippered salmon, use a lighter brine, dry alder with the bark removed, and less cooking time.

⌁ *Note: For complete information on how to smoke fish— the varied methods—see* Cooking Alaskan.

· ·

Rockfish with African Peanut Sauce

The Alaska Heritage Seafood Cookbook ⌁
ANN CHANDONNET

Simon & Seafort's Saloon & Grill in Anchorage regularly offers this rockfish entrée on its lunch and dinner menus.

Discriminating diners seem to welcome the contrast of the creamy peanut sauce with the bite of hot red chiles and lime. Serve with Pecan Wild Rice (page 178) or baked potato. This recipe can easily be halved.

- To make the Hot Pepper Oil, heat the olive oil and peppers in a saucepan until hot. Let the peppers stand in the oil for 10 minutes. Strain. Puree the olive oil, garlic, and salt. Reserve in a cool place.

- To make the Peanut Sauce, heat the clarified butter in a saucepan. Add the onion and garlic, and sauté until soft; do not brown. Add the tomatoes, peanuts, stock, salt, peppers, and lime juice. Simmer over medium heat until reduced by half. The sauce should be thick. Add the cream, and simmer for 10 minutes. Keep the sauce warm in the top of a double boiler.

- Preheat a stovetop or gas grill, or light coals. Oil the grill rack.

- Dip the fish in the Hot Pepper Oil. Remove any excess oil with your fingers.

- Place the fish skin side up on the grill at a 45-degree angle with the tail end (the thinner section) on the cool side. Grill for 2 minutes, until marks form. Baste with Hot Pepper Oil, and season each fillet with ¼ teaspoon of the steak salt.

- With a spatula, turn the fish 45 degrees in the other direction to form a diamond searing pattern. Press the spatula firmly against the grates to avoid tearing the surface of the fish. Grill for 2 minutes. Baste again with Hot Pepper Oil.

- Turn the fish over. The diamond markings should be facing up. Baste with the Hot Pepper Oil, and grill for 2 or 3 more minutes, or until done. The fish should be soft and moist. Season with the remaining steak salt.

- Place the fish on warmed plates, pouring about ⅓ cup of the Peanut Sauce over the center of each fillet. Leave the outer edges of the fish exposed, to show off the grill marks.

- Sprinkle 1 teaspoon of chopped green onion over each fillet, and garnish with a lemon slice.

MAKES 8 SERVINGS.

8   rockfish fillets, about
       7 ounces each
2½ teaspoons seasoned
       steak salt of your
       choice
4   green onions,
       chopped
8   lemon slices or
       wedges

Hot Pepper Oil

2   cups olive oil
2   teaspoons crushed
       red chile peppers
3   cloves garlic, minced
1   tablespoon kosher
       salt

Peanut Sauce

¼   cup Clarified Butter
       (page 200)
1   cup minced onion
2   teaspoons minced
       garlic
1   pound tomatoes,
       diced and drained
1   cup minced peanuts
4   cups chicken stock
2   teaspoons kosher salt
1 to 1½ teaspoons
       crushed red chile
       peppers
¼   cup fresh lime juice
1   cup heavy cream

Beluga whale meat on drying racks, Kotzebue.

Muktuk

Cooking Alaskan ∾ RECIPE BY HELEN HICKOX,
former teacher, Gambell High School, Saint Lawrence Island

*M*uktuk is the blubber and skin of whale. The black, thin layer of skin on white, pinkish blubber is *muktuk*. It is eaten just as it comes off the whale. It is cut in small strips, sliced thin, and eaten with salt. Some people use seasoned salt as well. Some say it tastes like coconut, but to me it tastes a lot like salt pork before cooking.
The only part used is the skin that covers the blubber.

Today my recipe will be making half-dried boiled salmon," Uto told her friends. "After the salmon has dried for three days, take down enough for a meal, and cut it into three-inch pieces. Put the pieces in boiling water. Let the half-dried fish boil until the raw part of the fish is done. Serve it on your fish platter with a side dish of greens and seal oil. That is my recipe."

—*The Storytellers' Club*, LORETTA OUTWATER COX

Mukluk Meat Loaf

Cooking Alaskan ~ RECIPE BY ELFIE APATIKI,
Community Education Program Cookbook,
Gambell, Saint Lawrence Island

1 pound chopped or
ground *mukluk* meat
1 egg or 3 tablespoons
powdered egg
1 cup rolled oats
¼ cup flour
1 cup canned peas
with juice
½ teaspoon salt
¼ teaspoon pepper

On Saint Lawrence Island, *mukluk* is giant or bearded seal. For the following recipe, the cook suggests rinsing the meat thoroughly and soaking it in salted water before it is ground. Use 2 tablespoons salt per gallon of water. Drain well, chop or grind the meat and proceed.

• Mix all ingredients thoroughly. Put in greased loaf pan. Bake for 20 to 30 minutes at 450°F. Walrus meat can be used in the recipe, but it requires longer baking, about 45 minutes.

To a devoted seafood fiend, the two-toned muktuk tasted like the smoothest sushi imaginable.

Munching off my sword-ke-bab and dripping whale oil, I examined the fully landed animal carefully, circling it. We had the relationship mixed up, it seemed to me for a second. This whale should be eating us.

Putting up [the whale meat] had just been the relatively easy first stage. Now we had to get the 46 tons into bite-sized, or at least boulder-sized packages. We were clearly into an all-night activity, at least. Which isn't too bad, when you consider that it's meat for four months, for everybody.

—*Not Really an Alaskan Mountain Man,* DOUG FINE

Four-Day Spiced Walrus

Cooking Alaskan 〜
Recipe adapted from *Walrus in the Cooking Pot*

Corned walrus—rated very good.

- Soak the meat in vinegar-water for about 10 minutes. Then take it out and wipe it dry. Mix the remaining ingredients in a bowl. Cut several slits in the meat and put some of the spice mixture down into the cuts. Rub the rest over the outside of the meat. Wrap the meat securely in heavy plastic and store it in a cold place, below 45°F but above freezing, for four days.

- Then wrap in foil tight enough that meat juices will not escape during cooking. Roast in an uncovered pan in a slow oven, 300°F for about four hours.

- Let the meat cool before slicing into serving pieces.

1	well-trimmed chunk of walrus meat, 6 to 8 pounds
1	gallon water to which ¼ cup vinegar is added
1	tablespoon garlic salt
1	tablespoon saltpeter
4	tablespoons plain salt
5	tablespoons allspice
5	tablespoons sugar
½	teaspoon cinnamon

Whale Meat

Cooking Alaskan 〜 RECIPE FROM HELEN FISHER
An Alaskan Cook Book, Kenai

- Take one whale and clean well. Strip off all of the whale fat, and soak meat in vinegar for a few hours. The meat is fine-grained, dark red, and looks as if it should taste like beef. For a quick whale dish, slice meat into thin slices and brown in vegetable oil. Then pour prepared barbecue sauce or mushrooms over the browned meat and simmer until tender. Don't cheat and use garlic—let the full rich whale flavor come through.

Curried Seal Roast

Cooking Alaskan ﹏
RECIPE BY MARY DUNCAN, ANGOON

1   seal hindquarter
1   teaspoon salt
Mixed pickling spices
1   large onion
3   cups water
1¼ cups vinegar
¾ cup flour
1   teaspoon curry
    powder
1   teaspoon ground
    ginger
1   teaspoon garlic
    powder

• Place hindquarter in roasting pan and sprinkle with salt and pickling spices. Slice the onion in rings and scatter over the roast. Cover and put into the oven at 400°F for 2 hours or more, depending on the size. When the roast is almost done, mix the vinegar, water, flour, curry, ginger, and garlic powder like gravy and pour it into the meat juices in the roasting pan and stir well. Then cover roast again and cook for another 15 to 20 minutes. Serve with rice.

MAKES 6 SERVINGS.

Rendered Seal Oil

Cooking Alaskan ﹏ RECIPE BY FELECTA TETPON

Cut the seal fat in strips and put in a large container. Let it sit till it renders. When it renders, it starts to smell, but the smell is the natural smell of seal oil. The rendering place shouldn't be too cold, but not too warm either. In Shaktoolik, it is cool enough so you don't have to worry about the seal oil. In Homer, the weather is warmer and some of my seal oil has spoiled. Pour off the oil and store it before all of it is rendered. Remaining fat still renders.

Years ago, my mother put the fat in a seal poke [a container made from a seal stomach or a sealskin]. My husband [ivory carver Eric Tetpon] and I had to learn how to make our own seal oil. I didn't watch how my mother did it enough. My parents told me to leave a hole in the seal poke so the air could come in and keep it fresh. Keep the seal poke in a cool place.

Seal Oil Dip

Cooking Alaskan ∾
KAA T'EIX (MARY HOWARD PELAYO),
Kaa T'eix's Cook Book, Mount Edgecumbe

The rendered seal oil (page 120) has many uses. The older genera-
tion never went without seal oil for cooking. They used it to add
flavor to the salmon, seaweed with salmon eggs, or diced clams,
dried cockles, and sea ribbons. They even added the oil to desserts
like mixed berries. It is especially used with dried fish. Dried fish is
what you call a finger food nowadays. You take the roasted dried
fish and hold it in your two fingers and dip it into seal oil. This is
good eating.

It was probably because the Tlingits dried so many of their
edible foods that they usually served seal oil with it. It was easier
to eat the food that way and so much tastier.

This was Mark's first bearded seal,
proving him a marriageable man, able to hunt well and provide for
a family. Before the seal party, all the blubber and meat had been
sawed into big hunks. The seal oil had been rendered and poured
into empty pancake syrup bottles and salad dressing jars. The guests
had brought plastic pails and kiddie sleds to carry home the hunks
and oil, and all the other gifts.

—*Place of the Pretend People,* CAROLYN KREMERS

Jellied Moose Nose

Cooking Alaskan ∽
Recipe from *The Hunter Returns After the Kill*

Jellied moose nose is a sourdough specialty known and enjoyed only in moose country. It is not easy to prepare, but, like head cheese, is a worthwhile delicacy.

• Cut the upper jawbone of the moose just below the eyes. Put it in a large kettle of scalding water and boil it for 45 minutes. Remove it and plunge it into cold water to cool. Pick the hairs from the nose as you would feathers from a duck (the boiling loosens them), and wash the nose thoroughly.

• Put the nose in a kettle and cover it with fresh water. Add a sliced onion, a little garlic, and pickling spices and boil it gently until the meat is tender. Let it cool overnight in cooking liquid.

• In the morning, take the meat out of the broth and remove the bones and cartilage. You will have two kinds of meat: the bulb of the nose is white and the thin strips along the bone and jowls are dark. Slice the meat thinly, pack it into a high-sided glass dish, and cover it with juice. You may add salt, pepper, or other spices to the juice if they are needed. Some people add vinegar to suit their own taste. Refrigerate. The mixture will jell, and when it is firm, can be sliced for cold serving.

Fried Gooey Duck

Cooking Alaskan ∽
From "Early Day Recipes," *Tsimpshean Indian Island Cookbook,* Metlakatla

• Shell and clean gooey duck thoroughly. Cut off neck. Pour boiling water over and scrape the skin. Slit one side of the neck to open flat. Slice main part of gooey duck in half. Dip gooey duck into beaten eggs with grated onion. Then dip into corn meal. Fry for three minutes on each side.

Ptarmigan Rice Paella

Cooking Alaskan ∾ RECIPE BY JOE RYCHETNIK, "Dining Along the Eskimo Coast," *Alaska Sportsman* magazine, April 1964

Use either spruce hen or ptarmigan and allow 1 per person.

• Skin and quarter the birds, shake the pieces in seasoned flour, and fry in bacon fat or other shortening until tender. Arrange meat around the rice on a serving platter.

• To cook the rice, heat butter in heavy skillet, add garlic and rice and cook, stirring constantly, until rice turns golden. Add hot chicken broth or bouillon and remaining ingredients and heat to boiling again, stirring occasionally to separate frozen vegetables. Cover, reduce heat, and cook until rice is tender and all liquid is absorbed, about 20 minutes.

MAKES 4 SERVINGS.

Rice
2	tablespoons butter
1	clove garlic, crushed
1	cup raw rice
2	cups chicken broth or bouillon
½	teaspoon saffron
2	teaspoons salt
1	jar mushroom buttons with juice
1	package frozen carrots and peas
1	tablespoon monosodium glutamate

Bird(s)
Spruce hen or ptarmigan

Starving is very painful, suffering, and sad, which makes you feel real sick," Martha told the student. "That is, the stomach's shrinking is very painful. Even if a person is a great hunter, if food is not available, the great hunter would starve. When animals and other living creatures were real hard to find, the two great hunters looked for other pieces that were left. When they found a small needlefish, they cut the needlefish in half and shared the needlefish. That was to fill their stomach."

Among Yup'iks, sharing wasn't a function of plenty, it was a function of survival. It was essential in the Arctic, and besides, sharing made people feel good.

—*Place of the Pretend People*, CAROLYN KREMERS

Fish on a Stick

Cooking Alaskan ⌒
Recipe from *Tsimpshean Indian Island Cookbook,* Metlakatla

2 pounds salmon steaks
1 green pepper, cut into 1-inch squares
10 small onions
1 cup oil
½ teaspoon oregano
½ teaspoon salt
½ teaspoon thyme
1 teaspoon pepper
½ teaspoon garlic powder

Cut salmon into 1-inch pieces. Place alternately on a stick: salmon, pepper, onion. Place stick in a shallow dish. Pour oil and seasoning over and let stand for 1 hour. Drain and put fish over hot coals for 4 to 6 minutes. Keep stick turning. Can tell when done; the fish will flake.

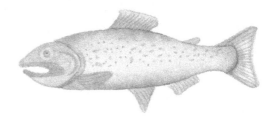

She thought about the commandment, "Thou shalt not steal." When she was little, she remembered her mother, Ekiyuq, talking with her about this. One fall, while they gathered food for the winter, they were out looking for a storehouse of the field mice. When they found one, they knew it would be full of musu, or wild potatoes, all bite-size and sweet. The mice knew when the musu had the best taste, and dug them up to store them for the winter. Her mother wouldn't take the whole store of wild potatoes from the mice, but left some, and even added some dried meat or fish in the place of the potatoes she took.

—*The Storytellers' Club,* Loretta Outwater Cox

Planked Fish

Cooking Alaskan ∼ RECIPE BY J. T. BROWN,
Port Edward, British Columbia,
"The Cabin Friend," *ALASKA* magazine, May 1976

A method of cooking that has long been used by Pacific
Northwest Coast Indians.

• Any fish can be planked. A plank or shake board can easily
be made with an ax from materials at hand, including your campfire wood supply. Almost any type of nonresinous wood can be
used; avoid cedar because of the heavy scent it gives off when
heated. Bark can also be used. Length and width of the plank is
governed by size of the fish to be cooked. Sharpen one end of the
plank for forcing it into the ground.

• Scrape the scales off fish and cut out gills. Leave head, fins,
and tail on. Slit the belly from vent to head. Remove viscera and
scrape kidney tissue from backbone. Split the back from the inside
so the fish can be opened wide as a book. Wash and pat dry. Wrap
fish line around the fish and plank to hold fish in place while cooking; have wedges handy for slipping under the line to keep the fish
tight and in place as it begins to shrink somewhat during cooking.
Putting the planked fish in campfire smoke for a time before cooking improves the flavor—but keep it away from the heat.

• Salt and pepper the prepared fish, tuck some thin pieces of
bacon or pork under the line at the top of the fish for basting.
Onion rings add flavor, too. Force the pointed plank into the ground
before a bed of hot coals, but not too close, or fish will scorch.
Catch drippings in a spoon and baste if you wish. Meat is done
when the flesh starts to curl and separate. Eat right off the plank.

Boiled Fish Heads

Cooking Alaskan ∾
Recipe from *The Alaska Dietary Survey*

Boiled fresh fish heads, especially those of the salmon and white-fish, are highly prized among Northern Eskimos. The cheeks and fat behind the eyes and the soft chewy cartilage are particularly well liked for their very delicate flavor. Occasionally, when cooking fresh salmon heads, some of the fresh salmon roe may be added.

▶ SARAH JOHN COOKING
FOR POTLATCH, VENETIE.

NATIVE TRADITIONAL FOODS

Bachelor Bannock, or Fry Bread

Cooking Alaskan ∾ RECIPE BY DICK PERSON,
Carcross, Yukon Territory

A recipe as generous as the size of your hand.

• Mix the first five ingredients in a medium bowl, using portions to suit your taste. Estimate the number of "cups" in the bowl and add baking powder accordingly. Mix well. Add milk powder and egg and mix again. Add enough water to produce a batter that is slightly wet, sticky, and light. It should fall slowly from spoon in a sticky mass. Then add nuts, raisins, and other goodies as desired.

• Put enough oil in the fry pan to completely cover the bottom. (Bear fat is the very best shortening to use. Corn oil is also good. Soya oil is bad.) Heat oil until a tiny amount of water dropped on the pan spatters and crackles.

• Pour batter in fry pan and fry until done. All the bannock mixture should be used at one frying or the baking powder gases will quickly escape and the remaining batter will lie lifeless in the pan.

3 handfuls whole wheat flour
1 handful wheat germ
½ handful of bran
½ to ¾ handful corn meal
¼ to ½ handful rolled oats (**Easy now. Too much will hold moisture and make the bannock soggy.**)
Baking powder, approximately 1 teaspoon per cup of the above ingredients
2 to 3 tablespoons milk powder
1 egg
Water
Nuts, raisins, dates (and so on) to taste
Oil or shortening

In the spring, the village became a festival of picking all kinds of greens, from sera, or willow, to ikuusuk, or wild celery; from fireweed, or kuppikutak, to wild rhubarb, or kunulik; from sourdock or kuagak, to Hudson's Bay tea (also called Labrador tea), or tilaakik; and so on. Once they brought the greens home, it was important to allow the leaves to rest and cool before they preserved them in fresh seal oil from the spring hunt. Sikki thought, it's like allowing the greens to have a grieving time before their spirits succumb.

—*The Storytellers' Club*, LORETTA OUTWATER COX

Agutuk, or Eskimo Ice Cream

Cooking Alaskan
ALICE SMITH, MEKORYUK, *Tundra Dreams*

1 cup beef, caribou, or moose fat
½ to 1 cup seal oil (sometimes *oogruk* [bearded seal] oil)
½ cup, more or less, water or snow
10 to 12 cups cloud-berries
0 to 2 cups sugar

If you use fresh seal oil you don't get the strong taste.

• Put a handful of Crisco in a bowl. Work it with your hand and add a little cold water. Put in the seal oil and work it more. The real Eskimo way was to make it with reindeer fat, chopped into small pieces. They put it on the stove to melt it. They never used to put sugar in. They used no sugar, just berries. Then later we used to put sugar in. Stir in the sugar. If you keep your hand working it a long time all the sugar melts, it dissolves. It will just fluffy up, now watch. You keep adding water, more water. Every time you put sugar in, it will fluff more. Keep working it and you can't smell the seal oil. Then put in the salmonberries. There should be blackberries, too. And then I put it up in my little freezer up there, let it cool off, and eat it. If you just want to have a little spoonful now, you may.

They also gathered . . . a certain willow that they would need for medicinal purposes. Qutuuq used it for pain when she had her menstrual period or when someone was getting a bad cold. It also helped relieve headaches and fevers. Qutuuq also collected some stinkweed. She picked about four bundles, tied their stems with rawhide, and had Kipmalook hang them from the ceiling in the food cache. Stinkweed was prepared as a paste and applied to any pain on the body; or if a strong medicine was needed for a bad cold, a liquid was made from its leaves and the sick person would drink this very potent concoction. Sometimes it worked, but not every time.

—*The Winter Walk*, LORETTA OUTWATER COX

As a boy I admired the knowledge and
abilities of many of the Koyukon elders, and I loved listening to their
stories of the past. I learned from them that during the 1800s the
Koyukuk valley was poorer in fish and game than other areas in
Alaska. In contrast, the Yukon River, with its great runs of salmon,
was considered a paradise. At the time, if you didn't kill, you didn't
eat; the people's very existence depended on fish and game, and they
hunted and/or fished year-round. They didn't farm or grow crops.
They harvested some berries and dried fish that they caught.

—Shadows on the Koyukuk,
SIDNEY HUNTINGTON WITH JIM REARDEN

Sea Cucumber Fritters

Cooking Alaskan
RECIPE BY CLARA PERATROVICH, *Foods from the Sea*, Klawock

Clara Peratrovich is from the village of Klawock on Prince of
Wales Island. Through a school program called Traditional Foods
in Science, she hands on her skill in the use of subsistence foods to
the village children, and in other demonstrations, such as a work-
shop sponsored by the Southeast Alaska Native Women's
Conference in Ketchikan, she shares her expertise with adults as
well. Some of her knowledge has been collected on videotape and
in booklet form by the Ketchikan Indian Corporation.

• Mix ground sea cucumber, eggs, celery, onions, bread
crumbs or pancake mix with seasonings. The mixture will be thick
enough to spoon onto a hot griddle. Fry until golden brown on
one side, turn and fry on the other side.

About 12 large yein
(sea cucumber),
cleaned and ground
2 eggs
3 stalks celery, ground
or chopped
1 small onion, ground
or chopped
1½ cups fine bread
crumbs or 1 cup
pancake mix
1 teaspoon salt
½ teaspoon pepper

Caribou parts on cache, Anaktuvuk Pass.

Caribou Meatballs with Rice

Lowbush Moose ∾ GORDON NELSON

This is a recipe that makes me appreciate the convenience of quick-cooking rice.

• In a medium-sized bowl, mix the meat, rice, onion, garlic, allspice, and salt. When well blended, shape the mixture into balls about the size of Ping-Pong balls.

• In a frying pan, mix the soup, water, and Worcestershire sauce, and bring to a boil. Carefully put the meatballs into the soup mixture, cover, and cook for 45 minutes over medium heat.

• Remove the meatballs to a platter and keep warm. I sometimes thicken the soup and turn it into gravy, which can be poured over the meat or served separately.

MAKES 4 GENEROUS SERVINGS.

1	pound ground caribou or beef
⅔	cup quick-cooking brown rice, uncooked
¼	cup onion, minced
1	clove garlic, minced
¼	teaspoon ground allspice
½	teaspoon salt
1	10½-ounce can tomato soup
1	cup water
1	tablespoon Worcestershire sauce

Riversong Moose Stew

The Riversong Lodge Cookbook ⌢ KIRSTEN DIXON

6 strips of bacon, cut
into pieces

2½ to 3 pounds moose
meat, cut into
1-inch cubes

Salt and freshly ground
pepper to taste

3 tablespoons
all-purpose flour

1 large onion, peeled
and coarsely chopped

2 cups dry red wine

1 cup homemade or
canned beef stock

3 tablespoons brandy

2 cloves garlic, peeled
and minced

½ teaspoon dried
marjoram

½ teaspoon dried thyme

Half an orange, washed

6 whole cloves

2 tablespoons unsalted
butter

3 large carrots, peeled
and coarsely chopped

½ pound mushrooms,
coarsely chopped

Many people who have visited the lodge over winter have tasted this stew. I like to serve it with white rice and corn bread. Moose meat is our favorite meat because of its lean texture and rich flavor. It is still difficult to acquire commercially. Beef can be substituted.

● Preheat the oven to 350°F.

In an oven-safe 3-quart casserole, cook the bacon over medium heat until brown. Remove the bacon with a slotted spoon, drain, and set aside.

● Sprinkle the moose meat with salt and pepper. Dredge it in the flour. Add the meat to the pan drippings. Brown on all sides over medium heat.

● Add the reserved bacon, onion, wine, stock, brandy, garlic, marjoram, and thyme. Stir until the sauce thickens and is bubbly. Stud the orange with the cloves and tuck it into the liquid. Cover the casserole and place it on the center rack of the oven. Bake for 2 to 2H hours.

● In a large skillet, melt the butter over medium heat. Add the carrots and mushrooms and cook until tender. Set aside. When the stew is done, add the carrots and mushrooms, cover, and return to the oven for 5 minutes. Remove the orange and discard. Serve immediately.

MAKES 4 TO 6 SERVINGS.

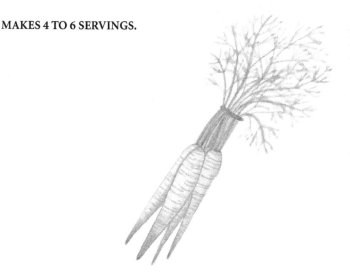

Cranberry Catsup Meat Loaf

Alaska Wild Berry Guide and Cookbook ∽

- Preheat oven to 375°F.
- Beat eggs in a large bowl; stir in the bread crumbs, onion, and green pepper. Gently mix in the meat and pork.
- In a small bowl, mix together the horseradish, salt, mustard, milk, and Highbush Cranberry Catsup; add this to the meat mixture.
- Shape the whole into a round loaf and place on a sheet of foil in a roasting pan. Bake for 45 minutes or until well browned and crusty. A few minutes before the dish is finished baking, drain cranberry sauce and spread over the loaf.

MAKES 6 OR MORE SERVINGS.

2 eggs
1½ cups soft bread crumbs
1 cup chopped onion
¼ cup chopped green pepper
1 pound ground moose or caribou meat
1 pound lean ground pork
2 teaspoons horseradish
¾ teaspoon salt
1 teaspoon dry mustard
¼ cup milk
¼ cup Highbush Cranberry Catsup (page 205)
1 cup cranberry sauce

Today I would carve a big wooden spoon for Mary Alsworth in exchange for the heavy boot socks. I dug out a likely piece of stump stock from the deep snow and went to work. She wanted a spoon with lots of curve so that is the way it would be. While I worked, the camp robbers kept me company. When they come a-begging, I always have time to feed them. They seem to have found the spruce buck perch to their liking. A kettle of beans simmered away on the fire, and when they were done, so was the spoon.

—*One Man's Wilderness*, SAM KEITH FROM THE JOURNALS AND PHOTOGRAPHS OF RICHARD PROENNEKE

Highbush Moose Pot Roast

Smokehouse Bear ❧ GORDON NELSON

4 pounds boneless rolled roast, beef or highbush moose

2 tablespoons vegetable oil

2 tablespoons all-purpose flour

1½ teaspoons salt

Pepper to taste

1½ cups beef stock (or 4 bouillon cubes and 1½ cups water)

2 cups chopped onion

2 cups fresh cranberries, lowbush or bog cranberry preferred

As I explained in my first cookbook, *Lowbush Moose*, the big, ugly, hairy creatures with the antlers are the real highbush moose. Lowbush moose are arctic hare or rabbit.

Likewise, cranberries grow on two levels in Alaska, highbush and lowbush. (You can guess where this is taking us.) You want the meat from the high bush and the berries from the low one for this dish. Or go buy a boneless rolled beef roast (as I did) and whatever fresh cranberries you can find.

● The 6-quart Dutch oven is the tool for this job. Set it on medium heat and add the oil. Wipe the meat with a damp cloth and rub on a mixture of flour, salt, and pepper. Brown the meat on all sides.

● Remove the meat from the pan and discard the pan drippings. Add the stock, onions, and cranberries to the pan. Return the meat to the pan, bring to a boil, and reduce heat to a simmer for 2H hours. Turn the meat once or twice during the cooking. When it's tender, remove the meat from the liquid and place onto a platter. Cover to keep warm.

● Skim the excess fat off the liquid in the pan. Pour the liquid into a blender, blend for 1 minute; then pour it through a strainer back into the pan. Reheat and add seasoning if needed.

● Slice the roast and arrange it on a platter. Pour the sauce over the meat and serve the rest in a gravy boat. Be sure to serve something else with the meat that demands gravy too.

SERVES 8 OR MORE.

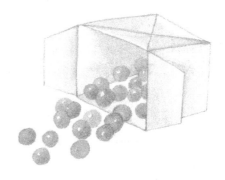

Russian America Borscht

Cooking Alaskan ᴖ
RECIPE BY THE EDITORS, *ALASKA* magazine

Borscht is one of those types of soups that may change every time you make it. Serve the soup hot or well chilled. Often the cold version is strained first, and only the flavorful broth is served. Add a generous spoonful of sour cream to the top of each serving and pass a bowl full of it too. Horseradish is another item that should be on the table for individualized seasoning. Rye bread, dill pickles, a soft spreadable cheese, and dark beer make good accompaniments.

• Brown bacon in bottom of Dutch oven or soup kettle until almost crisp. Spoon out bacon and drain on paper towel. Drain off all but about a tablespoon of bacon fat. Chop meat into 1-inch cubes, removing as much fat as you can. Brown it and the onions in hot bacon fat. Then add the beets, carrot, turnips, and bacon pieces. Sprinkle them with a teaspoon of flour and stir everything around to absorb the fat. Add stock, bring to a boil, cover, and simmer until meat is tender, about 1½ hours. If your soup kettle is ovenproof, you may bring the soup to boil on top of the stove, and then set it in the oven to continue cooking at about 325°F, 2 hours or more.

• When the meat is tender, add vinegar, sugar, shredded cabbage, and potato and cook 30 minutes longer, or until potato and cabbage are done.

• Measure tomato paste into a larger cup or bowl, add flour, and then thin the mixture with several spoonfuls of the hot soup, blending it well and then stirring it into the soup. Add salt and pepper to taste . . . more vinegar, if you want. Serve with sour cream as a garnish.

MAKES 8 SERVINGS.

2   strips bacon, cut in 1-inch pieces
1   pound lean moose meat or other game (beef, in a pinch)
1   large onion, chopped
2 or 3 raw beets, peeled and diced (about 1½ cups)
1   large carrot, diced
2   medium turnips, diced
1   teaspoon flour
2   quarts game or beef stock
¼   cup vinegar
2   teaspoons sugar
1   cup shredded cabbage
1   potato, cubed
2   tablespoons tomato paste
An additional teaspoon (or more) of flour
Salt and pepper to taste
1   pint sour cream

Rabbit and Reindeer Sausage Skewers

The Riversong Lodge Cookbook ∽ KIRSTEN DIXON

1 large rabbit (about 2½ pounds)
2 cups white vinegar
⅓ cup canola oil
¼ cup dried sage leaves
4 large sprigs fresh rosemary
Salt and freshly ground pepper to taste
1½ pounds Alaska reindeer sausage
1½ pounds zucchini
Olive oil, for brushing the skewers

I prefer wooden skewers, but I soak them in water so they don't burn over the fire. Metal skewers always seem to impart a metallic taste. Serve this entrée with brown rice topped with shredded cheddar cheese and a dollop of sour cream.

• Bone the rabbit meat and cut it into 2-inch cubes. Place the rabbit meat in a medium bowl. Add the vinegar and oil. Add ¼ cup of the sage leaves, crumbling them onto the rabbit. Remove the leaves from 2 of the rosemary sprigs and add the leaves to the marinade. Season the rabbit meat with salt and pepper to taste. Mix well, cover, and refrigerate for 6 to 12 hours. Drain the marinade from the rabbit meat. Cut the reindeer sausage into 2-inch pieces. Cut the zucchini into 2-inch pieces.

• On 8-inch skewers, alternate the marinated rabbit, zucchini, and reindeer sausage. Brush the skewers lightly with the olive oil. Remove the leaves from the remaining rosemary sprigs and sprinkle the leaves over the skewers. Grill the skewers until the rabbit meat is firm and white, about 10 minutes.

MAKES 4 SERVINGS.

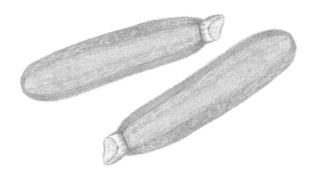

Marinated Venison Steaks

Cooking Alaskan ∿
Recipe from the *Northern Cookbook*

• Measure all ingredients into a jar that has a close-fitting top. Cover and shake vigorously. Pour into a large enamel, glass, or earthenware bowl, add steaks and allow to stand for several hours or overnight in a cool place.

• Remove steaks from marinade and drain well. Season with salt, pepper, and charcoal seasoning if desired. Rub preheated heavy frying pan with a piece of fat. Pan broil steaks quickly at high heat, turning every half minute until done. Do not overcook. Add only enough fat to prevent meat from sticking to pan. Serve sizzling hot.

MAKES 6 SERVINGS.

Marinade
¼ cup vinegar
2 tablespoons water
⅔ cup salad oil
1 tablespoon ketchup
1 tablespoon grated onion or dried onion flakes
1 teaspoon salt
½ teaspoon dry mustard
½ teaspoon sugar
½ teaspoon paprika
¼ teaspoon pepper
¼ teaspoon garlic salt

Steaks
6 venison steaks cut ½ to 1 inch thick
½ teaspoon salt
¼ teaspoon pepper
¼ teaspoon charcoal seasoning (optional)

Islander Venison Loin Chops

Cooking Alaskan ◞◞ RECIPE ANONYMOUS

1 small can (6 ounces) pineapple juice
2 tablespoons oil
2 tablespoons soy sauce
2 tablespoons lemon juice
2 cloves garlic, finely minced
⅛ teaspoon powdered clove
4 to 6 venison chops, 1 inch thick

• Combine all ingredients except chops in a screw-top jar and shake vigorously. Place chops in a glass baking dish and pour marinade over them. Cover and refrigerate for several hours or overnight, turning from time to time.

• Broil over coals or in a small amount of hot fat in a heavy frying pan, 5 minutes per side, or until done to your taste. The figure-conscious can omit the oil from the marinade with no loss of tenderizing power.

MAKES 4 TO 6 SERVINGS.

Caribou or Moose Meat Pie

Cooking Alaskan ◞◞ RECIPE BY THE OLD HOMESTEADER

1 pound caribou or moose round, cut thick
½ cup whole-wheat flour
Bacon drippings or other fat
Salt and pepper to taste
Hot water
1 large onion, cut in eighths
8 small potatoes or larger cubed spuds
(*continued* ➤)

For this dish, we usually prepare extra biscuits so that we will have some to eat with butter, too.

• Cut meat (other game, such as sheep, may be used, too) in large cubes, dredge in flour, and brown on all sides in drippings. Use a Dutch oven if possible or other heavy pan. Salt and pepper to suit. Cover meat with water and cook slowly until meat is tender. Add water from time to time to keep the water level constant. When meat is nearly done, add onions, carrots, and potatoes and cook until tender, about 20 or 30 minutes. At the end of the cooking, thicken the gravy with a flour and water paste, and add the peas, fresh or frozen. (At this point, you can change your mind and have stew with dumplings rather than meat pie. Prepare dumpling dough, drop by spoonfuls on top of hot stew, cover and continue cooking on top of stove until dumplings are done.)

• If you did not use a Dutch oven for the browning, now transfer the stew to a large baking dish. Otherwise use the Dutch oven for the last cooking, too. Preheat oven to 400°F. Roll out biscuit dough to about ½ inch thick. Cut the dough with a biscuit cutter and cover top of stew with biscuits. Bake 10 minutes, reduce heat to 350°F and continue baking until biscuits are a rich brown.

4	large carrots, cut in quarters
½	cup green peas, fresh or frozen, or more
1	recipe biscuit dough (or dumpling dough)

MAKES 4 TO 6 SERVINGS.

They had tracked the moose for a couple of days until they caught up with it and shot it. The moose hide was stretched out on the snow, and they were scraping both sides of it with a curved piece of trap spring tied to a short stick for a handle.

Chief John and his wife had banked the base of their tent with moose hair for insulation, and they had made a moose-hair bed for each of their five dogs. Chief John had found rocks at a nearby bluff with which to break the bones so they could boil out all the nourishing fat and marrow. They had skimmed the fat off the top of the water and with it made a soup. It was surprising how much fat they got out of those bones. I ate with them, and with a little added rice, that soup was delicious.

Some of the meat was cut into strips and dried into jerky. They cooked and ate all of the intestine parts and the large blood vessels. All the meat from the head (some of the sweetest meat on a moose) was removed, cooked and eaten. No usable part was wasted.

They were living real Indian style, enjoying life. They planned to consume the all-too-rare treat of fresh meat in leisure while basking in the warming spring weather. There was no need to hurry.

—*Shadows on the Koyukuk,*
SIDNEY HUNTINGTON WITH JIM REARDEN

Caribou Hot Pot

Cooking Alaskan ∿
Recipe from *Alaska's Game Is Good Food*

- Fill a medium-sized casserole with:

A layer of white potatoes, sliced ½ inch thick
A layer of tough lean caribou meat, cut small
A layer of sliced onions

- Mix and spread over casserole:

¾ teaspoon salt
¾ teaspoon paprika (or more to taste)
1 can (16 ounces) stewed tomatoes

- Cover and bake in moderate oven, 350°F, about 2 hours. Half an hour before the dish will be done, stir in ⅓ cup sour cream or yogurt.

MAKES 6 SERVINGS.

Roast Wild Goose with Apples

Cooking Alaskan ∿ A classic recipe from the *Tsimpshean Indian Island Cookbook,* Metlakatla

- Singe, clean, and wipe dry a young wild goose. Rub inside with salt and pepper. Peel and core four to six firm apples, depending on size. Where the core was removed, put 1 scant teaspoon brown sugar and 1 whole clove. Stuff the goose with these; sew up both ends, truss and brush with oil. Place breast up in roasting pan. Sear in a very hot oven for 20 minutes; then turn breast down and season with salt and pepper. Cover tightly; reduce heat to moderate and roast 1½ hours, possibly 2, or until tender. Baste occasionally with the broth that accumulates in the pan.

- The liver, heart, and gizzard should be put in a saucepan, seasoned with salt, covered with boiling water, and simmered until tender. When done, finely mince these giblets and save them for the gravy. To prepare the gravy, remove the finished goose from the roasting pan and place on a hot dish. Skim off all fat from the broth; then thicken with 2 tablespoons flour creamed to a smooth paste in 2 tablespoons melted butter. If too thick, add hot stock or boiling water to thin. Then add the minced liver, gizzard, and heart; season with salt and pepper and serve separately in a gravy boat.
- To serve the goose, untruss and garnish with 8 small slices of buttered toast that have been spread liberally with spiced apple butter. Sprinkle finely chopped parsley over the breast of the goose and send to the table.

MAKES 6 OR MORE SERVINGS.

Green Olive Marinade for Wild Goose

Cooking Alaskan ᴄ⁓ RECIPE FROM CLARENCE MASSEY, "To Cook a Wild Goose," *ALASKA* magazine, March 1973

- Mix the marinade ingredients, pour over meat and marinate, refrigerated, for 8 hours or more.
- Then place goose and about 3 cups of marinade into a Dutch oven. Cover and cook slowly for about 3½ hours at a low oven temperature, 325°F, or on top of the stove. Check occasionally to be sure there is sufficient moisture in the pan. Add more marinade or water if needed.

MAKES 6 OR MORE SERVINGS.

3 cups water
¼ cup brandy
½ cup stuffed green olives
2 carrots, grated
¼ cup olive oil
1 teaspoon salt
1 cup sherry
1 cup chopped onion
1 clove garlic, minced
¼ cup chopped celery leaves
2 tablespoons lemon juice
¼ teaspoon pepper
1 wild goose, cut into serving pieces

Roast Wild Goose with Apricot Stuffing

Cooking Alaskan
Recipe from *Game Birds from Field to Kitchen*

1 young wild goose
Juice of 1 lemon
Salt and pepper
¼ cup butter
¼ cup chopped onion
1 cup chopped
  tart apple
1 cup chopped
  dried apricots
3 cups soft
  bread crumbs
¼ teaspoon salt
⅛ teaspoon pepper
4 to 6 slices parboiled
  bacon
Melted butter

A "slow oven" bird with an excellent dressing.

• Sprinkle goose inside and out with lemon juice, salt, and pepper. Melt ¼ cup butter in a large saucepan, add onion, and cook until tender. Stir in apples, apricots, bread crumbs, salt, and pepper. Spoon stuffing lightly into goose cavity. Close opening with skewers and string. Cover breast with bacon slices and cheesecloth soaked in melted butter. Place goose breast up on rack in roasting pan. Roast at 325°F for 2½ to 3 hours. Allow 30 minutes per pound. Baste frequently with pan drippings. If age of goose is uncertain, pour 1 cup water in pan and cover during last hour of cooking.

MAKES 6 OR MORE SERVINGS.

Pan Roasted Spruce Grouse
with Lemon and Herbs

The Riversong Lodge Cookbook ⌒ KIRSTEN DIXON

At Riversong, spruce grouse, particularly hens, are favored at the lodge by European guests. The onion, lemon, and herbs in this recipe give the game bird a savory flavor. Substitute ptarmigan, partridge, or other grouse if you prefer.

● Preheat the oven to 400°F. Season the birds inside and out with the salt and pepper. Place wedges of onion and lemon into the cavity of each bird. Tuck the wing tips underneath the birds, and truss them securely with cotton string.

● Heat the olive oil and the butter in a large ovenproof skillet over medium heat until the butter mixture is hot but not brown. Put the birds in the skillet, breast side down. Sauté for 5 minutes, turning to lightly brown on all sides. Turn the birds breast side up. Add tarragon and chicken stock to the pan. Cover the skillet with foil and place in the oven.

● Roast until the juices of the thigh run pink, rather than red, when the thigh is pierced, about 35 minutes. Remove the birds from the skillet and cut in half. Discard the lemon and onion. Strain the pan juices and return to the skillet. Bring to a boil over medium-high heat and reduce the stock by half. Season to taste with salt and pepper. Place the birds on a warm serving platter and pour the stock over the birds. Serve immediately.

MAKES 4 SERVINGS.

4 large spruce grouse (about 1 pound each), rinsed thoroughly and patted dry
Salt and freshly ground pepper to taste
1 small onion, cut into wedges
1 small lemon, cut into wedges
¼ cup olive oil
2 tablespoons unsalted butter
1 tablespoon minced fresh tarragon, or 2 teaspoons dried tarragon
1 cup homemade or canned chicken stock

Pan-Fried Rabbit

Cooking Alaskan ～

2 rabbits cut in serving pieces
Salt and pepper
Lemon
Flour
Oil
Paprika

• Place portions on plate and rub all surfaces with salt; place in refrigerator for 12 hours. Wash off salt. Rub pieces lightly with cut lemon. Sprinkle with salt and pepper; dip in flour and fry in hot oil or shortening about ¼ inch deep in frying pan. Brown thoroughly and turn. When both sides are brown, cover, lower heat, and cook until tender. Sprinkle with paprika before serving.

MAKES 8 SERVINGS.

～ *Variations:*

(1) Gravy can be made from the drippings of pan-fried rabbit, just as you would make chicken gravy: Pour off all but a couple of tablespoons of fat, heat, rapidly blend in an equal amount of flour, and stir until foamy. Slowly add 1 cup or more of milk, stirring constantly until gravy is the thickness desired. Season to taste with pepper, salt, and garlic powder.

(2) Brown the meat as directed. Then place the pieces in a Dutch oven or covered casserole dish, add ½ cup water, cover tightly, and continue cooking on low heat or in the oven at 325°F for about 45 minutes. The moisture will tenderize the meat. The rabbit won't be "crispy," however.

(3) Brown the meat as directed. Then place the pieces in a Dutch oven or covered casserole dish, add the juice and tomatoes from a 1-pound can, chopped onion, and green pepper to taste, and swirl in ½ cup sour cream or half-and-half, or a small can of undiluted evaporated milk. Cover and bake in an oven reheated to 325°F for about 1 hour, uncovering the dish for the last 15 minutes.

Roast Rabbit with Potato Stuffing

Cooking Alaskan ⌒

Recipe from Alma Haik, *The Alaskan Camp Cook*

This recipe can be used with Dutch oven and campfire. Just cover the Dutch oven with coals and allow a little more cooking time.

• Make stuffing by combining all ingredients except bacon or salt pork and rabbit. Dress and wash rabbit, fill body with stuffing and skewer. Place in baking pan with legs folded under body and skewer in this position. Strip back of rabbit with bacon or salt pork to keep it from drying out. Roast at 400°F for 10 minutes, then pour on 1 or 2 cups hot water and cook 35 to 45 minutes. Shortly before the end of cooking time, take off the bacon and let the rabbit brown.

MAKES 4 SERVINGS.

2   cups mashed potatoes
2   tablespoons butter or margarine
1   teaspoon salt
½   teaspoon pepper
1½ teaspoons thyme or sage
1   cup chopped celery or 1½ teaspoons celery salt (if using celery salt, cut down on the table salt)
Bacon or salt pork
1   whole rabbit

We remembered the bear fat—that is, we heated it on a stove until it melted and could be poured into containers where it would keep fresh for months, especially when frozen. Pieces of dried fish dipped into melted bear grease is a delicacy eaten like potato chips. We also ate melted bear grease with low-fat fish and with lean game meats.

—*Shadows on the Koyukuk,*
SIDNEY HUNTINGTON WITH JIM REARDEN

Simple Oven-Dried Jerky

Cooking Alaskan
Recipe from *You and Your Wild Game*

5   pounds lean meat
    (game or beef)
3   tablespoons salt
1   teaspoon ground
    pepper
2   tablespoons sugar

• Trim as much fat as possible from the meat. Cut it with the grain into strips ½ inch thick, 1 inch wide, and up to 1 foot in length. Spread out meat and sprinkle on salt, pepper, and sugar. Then put the meat in a pan or dish and let it stand 24 hours in a refrigerator. If desired, the meat may be dipped in liquid smoke for a couple of seconds to add flavor.

• Spread out meat in the top half of a kitchen oven on a rack to dry. Open the oven door to the first or second stop. Heat at 120°F—the lowest temperature—for 48 hours or until the desired dryness is reached. Use an oven thermometer to make sure the oven does not get hotter than 120°F. Higher temperatures will result in hard, brittle jerky that crumbles when it is eaten.

Sourdough's Pemmican

Cooking Alaskan ᴄ⤳ RECIPE ANONYMOUS,
Courtesy of Mrs. Aline Strutz

A delicious blend of powdered jerky, dried fruits, sugar, and spices.

• To make the meat powder, start with jerky that has been made without seasoning, or cut long strips of lean meat—moose or caribou—as thin as possible and dry or dehydrate completely. When the meat is thoroughly dried, it must be pounded until it becomes powdered. If this sounds like too much work, simply run it through the meat grinder a couple of times using the finest blade.

• Melt the suet or bear fat and start to cook slowly, adding the jam or jelly as it simmers. In the meantime, blend the meat powder with soup stock, brown sugar, ground dried fruit, and spices and add this mixture gradually into the melted fat, stirring constantly all the while. Do *not* add salt unless the pemmican is to be used immediately. Cover tightly and place in the oven, which has been preheated to 300°F. Let bake for 3½ hours. Remove from oven, pour into shallow pans to cool and set. A little more hot soup stock may be added if the mixture seems too thick when it is poured.

• Ideal pans for cooling are individual foil pie pans as this size cake of pemmican is a good size to pack. Muffin tins make smaller blocks and can be filled to make thicker blocks. When thoroughly cooled and set, the cakes should be individually foil wrapped and stored in a cool, dry place until needed.

Put several small ones in your pocket when you start out for a day in the Bush. You will find these make mighty good eating. This pemmican is also a good emergency food to carry on any kind of a trip. It can be eaten "as is," fried like steak, or used in stew. Quite a versatile food isn't it? When you wish a hearty meal in camp, just open a can or two of beans, toss in a few cakes of pemmican, and stew until pemmican is dissolved in bean liquid. Make a batch of hot biscuits and you have a real feast.

4   cups powdered meat
1½ cups suet or bear fat
¾   cup lowbush cranberry jam, or wild currant jelly
½   cup soup stock
½   cup brown sugar
½   cup dried and finely ground blueberries, raisins, or currants
½   teaspoon each— savory, allspice, garlic powder, onion powder
1   teaspoon dried, minced, wild chives
¾   teaspoon black pepper

Horse and sled train with chicken.

Nelson's Oriental Chicken

Smokehouse Bear ⟋ GORDON NELSON

Way back in my youth, when I was serving as helper to a Chinese cook aboard a cannery tender, I watched him spread a mysterious special sauce over chicken pieces and then slide them into the oven. The chicken was delicious, but only recently did I discover what the sauce really was. Are you ready for this? It was only orange marmalade, prepared this way:

- In a small frying pan, melt the butter and sauté the onion until it is transparent. Add marmalade, take pan off the heat and stir.
- Place chicken pieces in a 13-by-9-by-2-inch baking pan that has been lightly greased. Sprinkle with salt and pepper. Spoon a small amount of marmalade sauce over each piece. Spread the remaining sauce on the larger pieces.
- Bake in a preheated 325°F oven for 1 hour or until the chicken is tender.

MAKES 4 SERVINGS.

2 tablespoons butter
1 large onion, minced
¼ cup orange marmalade
1 frying chicken, cut in serving pieces
Salt and pepper

Quick Chicken for Two

Tired Wolf  GORDON NELSON

2 tablespoons
vegetable oil
2 tablespoons butter
1 clove garlic, crushed
2 chicken breasts,
approximately
8 ounces each, boned
and skinned
Paprika
2 tablespoons dry
white wine
1 tablespoon lemon
juice
¼ teaspoon salt
Pepper
Lemon wedges
for garnish

This recipe has become a favorite on the nights that Connie and I are home alone. It's quick and easy.

• Use a 1-quart glass baking dish with a cover. Into the dish place vegetable oil and butter. Add garlic and slide the dish into a microwave oven, set on high, for a minute. Remove the garlic from the dish.

• Place both chicken breasts in the dish. Turn each piece once or twice to coat the meat with the oil. Cover and place dish in microwave again. Cook on medium-high for 3 minutes. Remove from the oven, turn the chicken breasts over, sprinkle with paprika, cover and return to the microwave oven for another 2 minutes at the same setting.

• Remove from the oven and combine the wine, lemon juice, and salt with the cooking liquid. Spoon over the chicken pieces. Return to the microwave for the final 2 minutes at the same setting.

• Remove from the oven and serve. I would suggest a bowl of hot brown rice over which you could pour the remaining—fantastic—cooking liquid. Pepper the meat and garnish with lemon wedges before serving, if you desire.

MAKES 2 SERVINGS.

Pecan Breaded Chicken with Honey Mustard Sauce

The Double Musky Inn Cookbook ∾
BOB AND DEANNA PERSONS

We serve the Pecan Breaded Chicken with Cajun Sausage Dressing (page 185) and a small dish of Honey Mustard Sauce.

• Preheat oven to 500°F.

• For the Honey Mustard Sauce, melt the butter/margarine blend in a saucepot on low heat. Once melted, remove from heat and add the mustard and honey, and mix using a whisk until well blended. Store in the refrigerator.

• Trim any fat or cartilage from the chicken breast and pat it dry with a paper towel.

• Next, coat the skin side of the breast with the Honey Mustard Sauce. The best way to do this is put some sauce on a plate or pie pan and lay the breast in it skin side down. It is important that the meat is dry or the sauce will not stick as well.

• In another pan, combine equal amounts of bread crumbs and chopped pecans (about ½ cup per chicken breast). Take the sauce-coated chicken breast and lay it down on top of the breading. Press it down firmly so the breading sticks to it.

• Put the chicken breasts breaded side up in the roasting pan or cookie sheet that has been coated with oil or nonstick cooking spray and bake it in the oven until it is done, 10 to 12 minutes. (If you are using a chicken breast that's more than ¾ inch thick, reduce the oven temperature to 400°F and cook the chicken a bit longer to be sure it is done. The reduced heat will prevent the breading from burning.)

MAKES 4 SERVINGS.

4 boneless breasts, 7 to 8 ounces each
1 to 2 cups Honey Mustard Sauce to coat
2 cups bread crumbs to coat
2 cups chopped pecans to coat

Honey Mustard Sauce
½ pound butter/margarine blend
1 cup Dijon mustard
1 cup honey

High Mountain Glazed Birds

Tired Wolf ∼ GORDON NELSON

¼ cup apricot juice
¼ cup soy sauce
2 tablespoons sherry
1 clove garlic, minced
1 tablespoon freshly
  minced ginger (or
  ¼ teaspoon ground)
4 game hens,
  Rock Cornish or
  ptarmigan, thawed
2 tablespoons butter or
  margarine, melted

Dressing

2 cups cooked brown
  rice
½ cup chopped celery
½ cup chopped onion
1 teaspoon dried
  parsley, crumbled
½ teaspoon salt
⅛ teaspoon pepper
¼ teaspoon ground
  thyme
¼ teaspoon ground
  mace
¼ teaspoon ground
  nutmeg
2 tablespoons butter or
  margarine, melted

The first time that I was served this dish, the bird involved was a ptarmigan from the high Talkeetna Mountains. Since obtaining the recipe, I've only had occasion to use it with Rock Cornish game hens. They are excellent! For festive occasions, I like to add things to the dressing, such as soaked dried fruit, nuts, mushrooms, and, to be really fancy, oysters.

● In a bowl create a marinade by combining the apricot juice, soy sauce, sherry, garlic, and ginger.

● Rinse birds carefully and pat dry. Place them in a shallow dish large enough to hold the 4 birds. Spoon the marinade over them. Refrigerate. It's best to give them up to 4 hours in the marinade, turning them several times.

● The dressing for the birds is created by combining the rice, celery, onion, parsley, salt, pepper, thyme, mace, and nutmeg in a large bowl. Add 2 tablespoons of melted butter to the mixture. Mix the contents of the bowl well.

● When cooking time arrives, divide the dressing among the 4 birds, secure the cavity, and truss the wings and legs. Place the

Today, since they were arriving in the middle of the day, she would serve them ptarmigan soup. She knew she would probably talk about last weekend, when she took her grandson along with her to catch ptarmigan. They had caught enough ptarmigan for the whole week. Sikki would ask her friends if they wanted to take some home. In fact, they had decided that today, they would be sharing recipes and sharing something about themselves.

—*The Storytellers' Club*, LORETTA OUTWATER COX

birds, breast side down, in an uncovered roasting pan. Brush with
the marinade just before slipping into a 350°F preheated oven.
For the first 30 minutes of the roast, baste the birds with marinade
every 10 minutes.

• Then turn the birds over with the breast sides up and brush
tops with 2 tablespoons melted butter. Continue to roast and baste
the birds every 10 minutes for the next 40 minutes. The birds should
be nicely browned and glazed. If the legs feel loose the bird is done.

• Serve a whole bird to each person.

MAKES 4 SERVINGS.

▼ Ptarmigan in a
snowy field.

Workers with cows, horse, and dogs at dairy in Nome.

Grilled Marinated Flank Steak

A Cache of Recipes ∾ LAURA COLE

Flank steak comes from the rear section on the underside of the animal. It is a very lean, thin, and tasty cut of meat, usually weighing around 2 pounds. The marinade used for this grilled steak helps to form a tasty glaze on the beef. To match the bold flavors of the marinade, we serve flank steak with Roasted Garlic Smashed Potatoes (page 181) accompanied by Seared Peppers and Onions with Molasses Balsamic Glaze (page 180).

• Trim all visible fat from the flank steak. In a small bowl, mix the remaining ingredients together. Pour into a glass or enamel casserole dish large enough to hold the flank steak. Set the flank steak in the marinade, cover, and refrigerate for 12 to 18 hours. Turn the steak once during the marinating time to ensure even flavoring.

• Heat a grill. Remove the flank steak from the marinade. Grill, uncovered, until well browned on one side, 2 to 3 minutes. Turn over the steak and grill on the second side until well browned, 2 to 3 minutes. Remove the steak from the grill and let it rest for 5 minutes. Slice thinly on a slight diagonal against the grain.

MAKES 4 SERVINGS.

1   flank steak, about 2 pounds
¼   cup orange juice concentrate
5   tablespoons soy sauce
¼   cup dark sesame oil
2   tablespoons crushed garlic
2   tablespoons grated fresh ginger

French Pepper Steak with Brown (Burgundy) Sauce

The Double Musky Inn Cookbook

BOB AND DEANNA PERSONS

Brown (Burgundy) Sauce

Stock
4 cups beef stock
Dash of Burgundy wine
Beef base to taste

Roux
½ pound butter/margarine blend
½ pound of flour, or more as needed, to thicken roux
(*continued* ➤)

This is the steak that the Musky is famous for. Select a well-marbled steak that is at least 1½ inches thick, like New York steak, and trim off any excess fat.

- To make the sauce, put the beef stock, wine, and beef base in a medium pot, one at least twice the size of the sauce you are making, and bring to a boil over high heat, then reduce the temperature to low and simmer for a minimum of 30 minutes or up to an hour.

- For the roux, as the stock is heating up, make a brown roux (see Note) with the butter/margarine blend and flour. Don't use whole butter as it will taste scorched in a brown roux. If you burn the roux even a little, start over.

- Remove the roux from the heat and let it cool a little, stirring it constantly. Add a little of the stock (about ¼ cup or so) to the hot roux to cool it down faster. When you do this, it will boil and bubble with a lot of steam, so be very careful.

- Preparing the sauce: Now comes the fun part. Move the stockpot off the hot burner before adding the roux to it (or else it will stick to the bottom). Very carefully add the hot roux to the stock a little at a time. Stir in the roux with a whisk and continue adding the roux until it is all in the stock.

- Put the sauce back on the burner and bring it to a simmer over low heat, stirring constantly with the whisk. The sauce should be thick enough to coat the back of a spoon; add more stock or roux to adjust consistency as necessary. Simmer the sauce on low heat for at least 1 hour to fully cook the roux and make a smoother sauce.

MAKES 4 TO 5 CUPS. BEST USED FRESH.

- To make the steak, mix together soy sauce and lemon juice.
- Mix together Brown (Burgundy) Sauce with ¼ cup of coarse black pepper.
- Mix together flour and ½ cup of coarse black pepper.
- Put about ¼ inch of corn oil into a hot cast-iron skillet and heat it until oil pops when a drop of water is dropped in it.
- Using tongs, dip the steak into the soy-lemon mixture, then into the flour mixture, coating it on all sides. Handle the steak gently so as not to knock off the flour crust. What you're aiming to do is to cook it on all sides, creating a crust. After coating, place the steak in the skillet. Turn the steak frequently, and if it's large, fry the sides too. You may have to hold the steak upright with the tongs to cook the sides. For a medium-rare steak, this will take about 10 to 12 minutes. After the first minute of cooking, make sure you raise the steak so that the hot oil runs underneath it. You want the pepper-flour crust to turn a golden brown on all sides. The crust will be darker if the steak is more than medium-rare in temperature.
- When the steak is cooked to your satisfaction, remove it from the pan and pat the excess oil off gently with paper towels.
- Place the cooked steak on a plate and pour the peppered Brown (Burgundy) Sauce over it.

Steak

4   New York steaks, 16 to 20 ounces each
2   cups soy sauce
¼   cup lemon juice
2   cups flour
¾   cup coarse black pepper
2   cups Brown (Burgundy) Sauce
Corn oil

MAKES 4 SERVINGS.

༄ *Note: We use roux to thicken and flavor many sauces at the Double Musky. To make the roux, melt the butter on high heat, and when melted, add a little of the flour, whisking it in. Keep whisking, adding more flour until it reaches the consistency of cooked oatmeal. Keep adding flour, and make sure the roux does not stick to the pan or it will burn. Let it continue to cook, stirring constantly. As it cooks, the roux will smooth out and turn darker. When it is a reddish chocolate brown, it is a brown roux, and can be used for the Brown (Burgundy) Sauce.*

Tenderloin Beef Stroganoff

The Winterlake Lodge Cookbook ～ KIRSTEN DIXON

1½ pounds beef tenderloin, cut into thin strips
2 tablespoons butter
2 cloves garlic, peeled and minced
1 tablespoon flour
1 pound mushrooms, sliced
1 cup beef broth
12 pearl onions
½ cup heavy cream
½ cup sour cream, at room temperature
2 teaspoons Dijon mustard
¼ cup finely chopped fresh Italian parsley
Salt and freshly ground Winterlake pepper blend (equal parts black peppercorn, white peppercorn, and allspice)

This dish is a favorite at Winterlake Lodge. It's an old-fashioned and internationally known dish, but our entire kitchen staff particularly likes our version with its touch of Dijon mustard and Italian parsley. We use beef tenderloin in the dish and serve it with buttery wide egg noodles—elegant as well as delicious.

● In a large sauté pan over medium-high heat, sear the beef. Remove the beef from the pan and set aside.

● Melt the butter in the sauté pan and add the garlic. Sauté for 1 minute, then add the flour and stir with a wooden spoon, cooking until light brown, about 2 to 3 minutes. Add the mushrooms and ¼ cup of the beef broth. Turn the heat to low, and simmer covered for 15 minutes.

● Meanwhile, bring a medium saucepan of water to a boil. Cut an X into the root end of each pearl onion. Drop them in the boiling water and boil for 5 minutes. Drain the onions and slip off their skins.

● Returning to the mushrooms, add the remaining ¾ cup of beef broth, the cream, sour cream, and mustard. Simmer for 5 minutes. Add the seared beef, the onions, and the parsley, and season with salt and pepper to taste.

MAKES 4 SERVINGS.

Broiled Lamb Chops with Feta Cheese and Roasted Garlic

The Riversong Lodge Cookbook ⤳ KIRSTEN DIXON

The roasted garlic can be made a day ahead of time. The garlic is also great served with Gorgonzola cheese on toast points with a hearty red wine.

● Preheat the oven to 350°F. Roast the garlic by cutting off the tops of the cloves and loosening the sides. Place the garlic in foil, and pour a little olive oil over the top, and cover with additional foil. Bake for 50 minutes, until the garlic is soft.

● Mash the garlic in a bowl. Add the feta cheese. Sauté the spinach and shallots in butter until the spinach is wilted, and add to the bowl. Add the bread crumbs, egg, and oregano. You may have to add a little stock or water to be able to form the mixture into a ball.

● Heat the broiler. Make a 1½-inch cut in the loin side of a lamb chop, down to the center bone, to make a small pocket. Fill with some of the garlic mixture. Repeat with the remaining lamb chops. Broil for 10 to 15 minutes, turning once. Serve immediately.

MAKES 4 SERVINGS.

3 large whole garlic bulbs
¼ cup olive oil
1 cup crumbled feta cheese
2 cups sliced spinach leaves
2 shallots, peeled and minced
2 tablespoons unsalted butter
1 cup fine sourdough bread crumbs
1 egg
½ teaspoon dried oregano
8 lamb chops (1 to 1½ inches thick)

Grilled Pork Tenderloin with Caramelized Apples and Maple Mustard Sauce

A Cache of Recipes ∽ LAURA COLE

Brine

4 cups water
¼ cup kosher salt
¼ cup maple syrup
¼ cup brown sugar
1 clove garlic, sliced
2 sprigs rosemary
3 sprigs thyme
1 bay leaf
1 teaspoon anise or fennel seeds
1 tablespoon juniper berries

Caramelized Apples

2 medium Granny Smith apples
2 tablespoons butter, melted
1 teaspoon kosher salt
1 teaspoon freshly ground pepper
¼ cup dried cranberries

Pork

2 pork tenderloins, 12 ounces each, brined in Basic Brine
¼ cup olive oil
2 teaspoons freshly ground pepper
(*continued* ➤)

This dish has a decidedly autumn flair. Grilling caramelizes the sugar infused into the pork from the brine, giving it great flavor and color. We serve this pork tenderloin entrée over wilted greens or lightly dressed spinach and wild rice cakes.

Basic Brine for Pork Tenderloin

Always make sure there is enough brine to completely cover the meat. Weigh down the meat, if necessary to keep it from floating.

• In a large stockpot over medium-high heat, bring the water to a boil. Add the salt, maple syrup, and brown sugar. Reduce the heat and simmer until the sugar and salt are completely dissolved. Remove from the heat. Add the garlic, rosemary, thyme, bay leaf, anise or fennel seeds, and juniper berries. Cool completely. When cool, transfer to a noncorrosive container. Add the meat to the brine and refrigerate for 12 to 14 hours.

MAKES 4 CUPS.

• To caramelize the apples: Preheat the oven to 400°F. Peel, core, and slice each apple into 12 wedges. Toss the slices in the melted butter, and season with salt and pepper. Spread the apple slices on a sheet pan, and bake for 12 minutes, until slightly golden. Remove from the oven and transfer to a medium bowl. Toss together with the dried cranberries, and set aside.

• To grill the pork: Light a grill. Remove the tenderloins from the brine. Rinse well under cool running water, and pat dry with paper towels. Trim all fat and silver skin from the pork. Coat with the olive oil, and season with pepper and chopped rosemary. Grill for a few minutes on each side. In a small bowl, combine the maple syrup and mustard. When the tenderloins are seared on all sides, brush them with the maple mustard mixture to coat. Loosely tent foil over the tenderloins and continue grilling until the internal temperature reaches 145°F. Allow to rest for 5 minutes before slicing.

To serve, slice the pork and serve with the Caramelized Apples and Maple Mustard Sauce and garnished with rosemary sprigs.

MAKES 6 SERVINGS.

• To make the mustard sauce: In a saucepan, heat the olive oil over medium-high heat, add the shallots, and sauté until golden. Add the thyme and pepper. Deglaze the pan with the white wine. Cook until the wine is reduced by half, and add the chicken stock. Reduce the heat to a simmer, and gently whisk in the maple syrup and mustard. Taste and adjust the seasonings. When ready to serve, whisk in the softened butter and serve.

MAKES 6 SERVINGS.

2 tablespoons chopped fresh rosemary
2 tablespoons maple syrup
1 tablespoon Dijon mustard
1 cup Maple Mustard sauce (recipe follows)
6 small sprigs rosemary

Maple Mustard Sauce

1 teaspoon olive oil
2 tablespoons minced shallots
1 tablespoon chopped fresh thyme
2 teaspoons freshly ground pepper
2 tablespoons white wine
1 cup double-strength chicken stock
2 tablespoons maple syrup
1 tablespoon Dijon mustard
2 tablespoons butter, softened

According to the books we're burning about 680 calories an hour per hundred pounds of body weight. We take turns breaking trail, and fantasize about our favorite trapline dinner, macaroni and cheese with hot dogs. Neither of us usually eats meat, except wild, but out here hot dogs are irresistible. Kept frozen in a tree, then sliced and tossed with boiling macaroni, the buttons swell to twice their size. Tonight they'll explode in our mouths peppery bursts of protein and grease."

—*Place of the Pretend People*, Carolyn Kremers
(talking about the grueling Wilderness Classic Race)

Baked Easter Ham

Alaska Wild Berry Guide and Cookbook ∽

1   ham
1   cup lowbush cranberry syrup or other berry syrup or jelly
1   teaspoon cloves
1   teaspoon nutmeg
1   teaspoon allspice
1   teaspoon dry mustard
½   teaspoon black pepper
½   cup orange juice
2   tablespoons dried orange bits or grated orange peel
½   cup hot water

• Skin ham and remove any excess fat. With a sharp knife make holes into the ham 2 inches from one another and as deep as the bone. Do this on all sides. Boil the remaining ingredients together until syrup is made. Force 1 tablespoon of this hot syrup into every hole in the ham, then place the ham in a large roasting bag. Place into a roaster. Pour half the remaining syrup over the ham, then close the bag piercing several small holes in its upper side. Bake in a 325°F oven for 18 minutes for each pound of ham. Brown the meat by slitting open the bag 30 minutes before it's through cooking. Pour the remaining syrup over the ham and finish baking.

MAKES 6 OR MORE SERVINGS.

Fresh meat and wholesome water and the bulbs and roots gathered by Steller were showing their effects, and the scurvy epidemic had been checked. The sick were slowly regaining their strength, many could stand again and walk without support, and their teeth grew firm enough to chew the tough and sinewy otter flesh.

—*Where the Sea Breaks Its Back,* COREY FORD

Crusty Baked Ham

The Riversong Lodge Cookbook ⮑ KIRSTEN DIXON

Usually my girls don't care much for mustard, but they love this ham, sliced thin and served with mashed potatoes.

• Place the ham in deep, ovenproof casserole. Add the cider and Calvados. Cover and refrigerate overnight, turning the ham occasionally.

• Remove the ham from the refrigerator and let it warm to room temperature. Preheat the oven to 350°F. Remove the ham from the marinade, reserving the liquid, and pat dry. Spread the ham with the mustard, reserving 1 tablespoon. Mix the bread crumbs and brown sugar together. Roll the ham in the bread crumb mixture to coat thoroughly.

• Put the ham in a roasting pan and bake 1 hour, or until golden and heated through. Let rest 15 minutes before serving. Meanwhile, place the reserved marinade in a small saucepan and boil over high heat until it is reduced by half. Whisk in the vinegar and the remaining 1 tablespoon mustard. Serve the sauce with the sliced ham.

MAKES 6 TO 8 SERVINGS.

1 boneless smoked ham (about 5 pounds)
4 cups apple cider
1 cup Calvados or applejack
1 cup Dijon mustard
2 cups sourdough bread crumbs
½ cup light brown sugar
1 tablespoon apple cider vinegar

Spambalaya (Jambalaya)

Hibrow Cow ～ GORDON NELSON

This is a recipe I put together one night long ago, when I had a limited meat supply. I've had occasion to make it many times but

▶ MAN STANDING ON LADDER
AT FOOD CACHE IN
SOUTHCENTRAL ALASKA.

I must admit, seldom exactly the same. It lends itself to changes. It's always tasty. You may substitute ham for SPAM® or make the meat a cup of sliced salami strips. And if you're like me, add a can of mushrooms to the dish.

• Start with a large frying pan or even better, a Dutch oven. Over medium heat, melt butter and sauté celery, onions, and garlic. When the onions are tender, add water, salt, parsley, thyme, bay leaf, tomatoes, and pepper. Stir carefully, add rice and stir again.

• Cover and cook over low heat for 30 minutes. Dice SPAM® into ½-inch cubes and add to pan. Continue cooking another 10 to 15 minutes, until rice is done.

• Remove from heat. Take out bay leaf and serve.

MAKES 4 TO 6 SERVINGS.

2	tablespoons butter or margarine (or vegetable oil)
2	cups chopped celery
1	cup chopped onions
2	garlic cloves, minced
2½	cups water
1	teaspoon salt
½	teaspoon dry, crumbled parsley
¼	teaspoon crumbled or ground thyme
1	bay leaf
1	can stewed tomatoes, Italian or regular
	Pepper
1	cup uncooked rice
1	can pork luncheon meat (SPAM®)

For better or for worse, there is now a Hormel-sponsored SPAM® recipe contest at every State Fair in the U.S. The Alaska State Fair at Palmer is famous for the rugged snowcapped peaks that surround the fairgrounds and for the huge 70-pound cabbages that grow during the daily 19 hours of summer sun . . . and there is also a SPAM® recipe contest.

Forty-two guys entered the contest, and they did everything with SPAM®: Enchiladas, pâtés, cannelloni, egg rolls, turnovers, omelets, kabobs, meatballs, dumplings, ice cream, cakes, pies, stir-fries, salads, spaghetti, spreads, and dips. The nouvelle SPAM® with goat cheese and sun-dried tomatoes would have won hands down, except it looked like roadkill swimming in motor oil.

The "Spammon Spread" combining salmon and SPAM® in a fish-shaped pâté was divine. The SPAM® gyozas were to die for. And the judges all agreed on the ultimate surprise—mincemeat rum-flavored SPAM® truffles won the 1994 contest unanimously!

—*Mr. Whitekeys' Alaska Bizarre,* MR. WHITEKEYS

Upper Tonsina Roadhouse garden.

Ms. Watts's Lentil Supreme

Hibrow Cow ∾ GORDON NELSON

The woman who offered me this recipe wished to remain unknown, but would accept Watts as an alias as long as I preceded it with Ms. She was blonde, with blue eyes and much more. The Tired Wolf had a momentary flash of rejuvenation, which faded all too fast. When she was gone, I managed to read the recipe. I had to try it. I hope you will, too. Leftovers can be reheated. Like so many dishes, this seems to improve with time to mature.

- In a small bowl combine cayenne, paprika, ginger, cardamom, garlic powder, salt, coriander, cinnamon, vinegar, and 2 tablespoons water. Mix into a smooth paste and set aside.
- In a 5-quart pan over medium heat, sauté onions in oil for about 5 minutes. Stir in tomato paste and spice-bowl contents. Add ½ cup of water and cook for another 5 minutes, stirring.
- Add remaining 5 cups of water and lentils. Bring mixture to a boil and reduce heat to simmer. Cook, covered, for 45 minutes, occasionally stirring. Test lentils. They should be soft to the bite. Add cooking time only if needed, and in small amounts.
- Serve in bowls while still hot. Place slices of lime or lemon beside each bowl.

MAKES 6 TO 8 SERVINGS.

¼	teaspoon cayenne
1	teaspoon paprika
½	teaspoon ground ginger
½	teaspoon ground cardamom
¼	teaspoon garlic powder
¼	teaspoon salt
⅛	teaspoon ground coriander
⅛	teaspoon ground cinnamon
2	teaspoons white vinegar
2	tablespoons water
2	large onions, chopped
¼	cup vegetable oil
⅓	cup tomato paste
5½	cups water
2	cups lentils
2	limes, cut in wedges (lemons okay)

Spicy Black Bean Cakes

A Cache of Recipes ～ LAURA COLE

1 cup dried
 black beans
6 cups rich vegetable
 stock
6 scallions, thinly
 sliced
½ cup diced red
 bell pepper
½ cup chopped
 fresh cilantro
1 tablespoon
 minced garlic
1½ teaspoons minced
 jalapeño chile
1 tablespoon ground
 cumin
1 tablespoon
 kosher salt
2 eggs
¼ cup bread crumbs
1 cup yellow cornmeal
6 tablespoons olive oil
2 large avocados,
 peeled and pitted,
 each cut into 9 slices
6 tablespoons
 sour cream
18 sprigs of cilantro

The avocado and sour cream help cool the spiciness of these little cakes. Cooking the black beans in a rich vegetable broth infuses them with flavor.

• Soak the beans overnight covered in cool water. Rinse the beans well and drain. Transfer to a large heavy-bottomed stockpot and add vegetable stock to cover. Bring to a boil over medium-high heat. Reduce the heat and simmer until the beans are cooked tender, about 45 minutes. Drain and rinse under cool running water.

• Place the drained beans in a large bowl. Using a potato masher, mash the beans coarsely. Add the scallions, red bell pepper, cilantro, garlic, and jalapeño. Stir to combine well. Season with the cumin and salt, stirring to combine. Mix in the eggs, stirring to combine. Add the bread crumbs to form a dough. Place the cornmeal in a shallow bowl.

• Scoop out 2 tablespoons of the bean mixture and drop it into the cornmeal, turning to coat. Shape into a cake and repeat with the remaining bean mixture, making a total of 18 cakes.

• Preheat the oven to 250°F. In a large skillet, heat 3 tablespoons of the oil over medium-high heat. When the oil is very hot, start frying the bean cakes, working in batches. Fry for about 5 minutes per side. Drain the bean cakes on paper towels and transfer to a shallow baking dish. Keep them warm in the oven while frying the remaining cakes.

• Serve the bean cakes warm on slices of avocado, topped with a dollop of sour cream. Garnish with cilantro sprigs.

MAKES 18 CAKES, 6 SERVINGS.

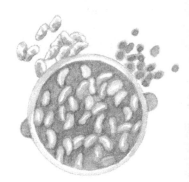

Eggplant Napoleons

A Cache of Recipes ⤳ LAURA COLE

It is important to look for eggplant with a tight, dark skin that is free of blemishes. For this recipe, look for long, thin eggplant rather than the huge, pear-shaped variety.

• Preheat the over to 450°F. Brush 2 sheet pans with some of the olive oil. Arrange as many of the vegetables as possible in a single layer in the pans. Brush the vegetables with some of the olive oil and season with salt and pepper. Roast the vegetables in the lower third of the oven until just tender and lightly browned, 10 to 15 minutes, rotating the pans halfway through. Transfer the roasted vegetables to a tray, arranging them by type in a single layer to cool. Roast the remaining vegetables in the same manner.

• In a small bowl, stir together the ricotta and thyme. Season with salt and pepper.

• Put 1 eggplant slice on a lightly oiled sheet pan. Spread 1 tablespoon of the ricotta mixture over the eggplant, top with 2 potato slices and then layer with 2 zucchini slices, 1 onion slice, 1 mozzarella slice, 2 tomato slices, 2 zucchini slices, and 1 additional onion slice. Spread a second tablespoon of ricotta mixture over the last layer of onion, and top with 1 eggplant slice. Secure the tower with a bamboo skewer.

• Repeat the process with the remaining vegetables, forming 5 more towers. Return to the oven for 5 minutes, until the vegetables are heated all the way through and the cheese has melted.

• Trim the rosemary sprigs so that they are 1 inch taller than the Napoleons, and remove the bottom leaves from the sprigs, leaving about 1 inch of needles around the top. After removing the Napoleons from the oven, remove the bamboo skewers and replace them with the rosemary sprigs to serve.

MAKES 6 SERVINGS.

½ cup olive oil
1 pound Japanese eggplant, cut crosswise into ⅓-inch slices
1¼ pounds zucchini, cut crosswise into ⅓-inch slices
4 large plum tomatoes, cut lengthwise into ⅓-inch slices
2 red onions, cut into ⅓-inch slices
1 pound red potatoes, cut into ⅓-inch slices
Kosher salt
Freshly ground pepper
1 cup ricotta cheese
1½ teaspoons fresh thyme
8 ounces mozzarella, cut into ¼-inch slices
6 sprigs rosemary

Vegetarian Lasagna

A Cache of Recipes ∽ LAURA COLE

Sauce

- 1 tablespoon olive oil
- 1 yellow onion, minced
- 2 cloves garlic, minced
- 1 green bell pepper, minced
- ¼ cup chopped celery leaves
- ½ cup chopped fresh parsley
- 2 cups prepared tomato sauce
- 2 large tomatoes, diced
- 1 (6-ounce) can tomato paste
- 2 teaspoons dried oregano
- 2 teaspoons dried basil
- 1 bay leaf
- ½ teaspoon freshly ground pepper
- 2 teaspoons salt
- ⅛ teaspoon cayenne
- 1 teaspoon Worcestershire sauce

For the best flavor, we recommend making the sauce a day ahead.

● To make the sauce: In a large saucepan, heat the oil over medium-high heat. Add the onion, garlic, and bell pepper. Sauté until aromatic. Stir in the celery leaves and parsley. Sauté until aromatic. Reduce the heat and stir in the tomato sauce, diced tomatoes, tomato paste, oregano, basil, bay leaf, pepper, salt, cayenne, and Worcestershire sauce. Simmer until very thick, up to 4 hours. Taste and adjust the seasonings. Cool and refrigerate until ready to use. Remove the bay leaf before using.

● To assemble and bake lasagna: Preheat the oven to 350°F. Lightly grease a deep-sided 9-by-13-inch baking dish, or extend the sides of a shallower pan with a double thickness of greased aluminum foil.

● Spoon ⅓ of the sauce in the bottom of the dish, and top with a layer of uncooked lasagna noodles. Spread the ricotta cheese evenly over the noodles, and top with the spinach, mushrooms, and zucchini. Spoon ⅓ of the sauce over the top, and layer with the remaining noodles. Cover the noodles with the grated Monterey Jack and mozzarella cheeses. Top with the carrots and olives. Spoon the remaining sauce on top. Cover loosely with greased aluminum foil. Bake for 45 minutes, remove the foil, and continue to bake for an additional 30 minutes. Remove from the oven and top with the Parmesan cheese. Bake for 15 more minutes, until the cheese is golden brown and the sauce is bubbly. Remove the pan from the oven, and allow the lasagna to set for at least 15 minutes before cutting.

MAKES 12 SERVINGS.

Lasagna

1 (8-ounce) package small, wavy lasagna noodles
2 cups ricotta cheese
1 pound spinach, cooked and well drained
2 cups sliced fresh mushrooms
1½ cups sliced zucchini
8 ounces Monterey Jack cheese, grated
8 ounces mozzarella cheese, grated
1 large carrot, peeled and grated
½ cup sliced black olives
1 cup grated Parmesan cheese

◄ Mrs. Silverman and one of her cabbages, Anchorage.

Crustless Spinach Pie

The Riversong Lodge Cookbook ～ KIRSTEN DIXON

1 cup finely
   chopped onion
1½ cups sliced wild
   mushrooms
1½ cups sliced summer
   squash (a variety of
   types, preferably)
1 clove garlic, peeled
   and minced
3 tablespoons
   canola oil
5 eggs
2 cups ricotta cheese
1 tablespoon
   fresh thyme
3 cups fresh spinach,
   blanched, drained,
   and chopped
½ cup feta cheese,
   crumbled
Salt and freshly ground
   pepper to taste

We make different pies for lunches at the lodge. Europeans are delighted with this dish. Adapt the recipe for a river trip by preparing the pie in a large cast-iron skillet over the camp stove.

• Preheat oven to 350°F. Grease a 10-inch springform pan.

• In a large skillet, sauté the onion, mushrooms, squash, and garlic in the oil until softened, about 10 minutes. Combine the eggs and ricotta cheese in a large bowl. Beat until well blended. Add the sautéed vegetables, thyme, spinach, and feta cheese. Season the mixture with salt and pepper. Pour into the prepared springform pan. Place on the center rack of the oven and bake for 1 hour or until set. Serve in wedges.

MAKES 8 SERVINGS.

Vegetable Hash Baked in a Skillet

The Riversong Lodge Cookbook ～ KIRSTEN DIXON

We serve this hash as a breakfast dish or as a vegetarian main dish at other meals. We modify the ingredients according to the season.

• Heat 3 tablespoons of the butter in a large, ovenproof skillet over medium heat. Add the onion and sauté until soft, about 10 minutes. Add the garlic, carrot, potato, and chicken stock to the skillet. Cover and braise the vegetables until tender and the liquid is absorbed, 6 to 8 minutes. Remove 1 cup of the vegetable mixture and set aside. Add the red pepper, mushrooms, and basil to the skillet. Continue to cook uncovered for an additional 5 minutes, tossing the vegetables gently to mix.

• Preheat the oven to 450°F.

• Puree the reserved 1 cup of vegetables, the egg, and the cream in a food processor until almost smooth. Scrape into a large bowl. Add the vegetables from the skillet to the bowl. Season to taste with salt and pepper.

• Heat the remaining 3 tablespoons butter in the same skillet over high heat. Add the vegetable mixture, spreading it evenly in the bottom of the skillet. Cook for 2 to 3 minutes over medium-high heat. Bake in the oven until browned, 10 to 15 minutes.

• Heat the broiler. Sprinkle the cheese over the hash. Broil until browned, 1 to 2 minutes. Cut the hash into wedges and serve immediately.

MAKES 4 TO 6 SERVINGS.

6 tablespoons unsalted butter
1 large onion, peeled and diced
2 cloves garlic, peeled and minced
1 large carrot, peeled and diced
1 large potato, diced
⅓ cup homemade or canned chicken stock
1 red bell pepper, diced into ½-inch pieces
1 cup sliced wild mushrooms
¼ cup fresh basil, finely chopped
1 egg
3 tablespoons heavy cream
Salt and freshly ground pepper to taste
½ cup grated white cheddar cheese

▲ A WOMAN DRIVING
A TRACTOR, TETLIN.

Spicy Fried Zucchini

The Double Musky Inn Cookbook ∽
BOB AND DEANNA PERSONS

4 or 6 medium zucchini
2   cups flour
2   tablespoons
    Pasta Spice
8   eggs
Splash of milk
2   cups Seasoned Bread
    Crumbs plus extra
Oil for deep frying
Horseradish Sauce
    (*continued* ➤)

• Peel the zucchini and cut off both ends. Cut the zucchini in half crosswise, then split each half into wedges about ½ to ¾ inch thick. You want to end up with pieces the size of thick French fries.

• Mix the flour and Pasta Spice together in a small bowl. Mix the eggs and milk together in another small bowl. Put the Seasoned Bread Crumbs in a third small bowl.

• Next, bread the zucchini, using one hand for the dry breading and the other hand for the egg wash. First, dip the wedges into the seasoned flour and shake off the excess, then dip them into the egg wash and shake them around so that they are fully coated, then place them on the bread crumbs and cover them with more crumbs. Gently shake the bowl so that the zucchini wedges roll in the crumbs and are coated.

- Place the zucchini on paper towels; be gentle as the coating will easily brush off.
- Deep-fry the zucchini in oil preheated to 375°F until they are dark brown; drain on more paper towels to soak up any excess oil.
- Serve immediately with Horseradish Sauce.

MAKES 2 TO 4 SERVINGS.

- For Pasta Spice: Mix pasta spice well and store in sealed container. Makes approximately 1½ cups.

- For Seasoned Bread Crumbs: Fill a food processor bowl (metal blade installed) with the bread crumbs. Add the rest of the ingredients and process until mixed. You can also mix the bread crumbs by hand in a bowl, but some of the spices may settle if the crumbs are not mixed up again before use. Store in the refrigerator for up to 1 month.

- For Horseradish Sauce: Mix together horseradish sauce and store in refrigerator.

MAKES 2½ CUPS.

Pasta Spice

1	teaspoon ground bay leaves
1	cup paprika
1	tablespoon oregano
1	tablespoon basil
1	tablespoon thyme
3	tablespoons granulated garlic
3	tablespoons granulated onion
7	tablespoons salt
1	tablespoon black pepper
3	tablespoons cayenne pepper
3	tablespoons white pepper

Seasoned Bread Crumbs

5½	cups dry bread crumbs
6	tablespoons oregano
6	tablespoons finely grated Parmesan cheese
6	tablespoons parsley flakes
½	cup Pasta Spice

Horseradish Sauce

1	pound sour cream
5	tablespoons prepared horseradish
1	tablespoon lemon juice

Heady homestead vegetables, Matanuska Valley.

Winter Squash with Cranberries

Cooking Alaskan
RECIPE BY MAMIE JENSEN, JUNEAU

• Heat oven to 400°F. With egg beater, whip the squash with eggs and 3 tablespoons of the butter. Stir in sugar, cranberries, salt, and pepper. Spoon into 2-quart casserole, top with remaining butter, sprinkle with nutmeg. Bake uncovered, 30 to 40 minutes.

MAKES 8 SERVINGS.

4   cups cooked, mashed squash
2   eggs, beaten
⅓   cup melted butter
¼   cup granulated sugar
1½ cups raw lingonberries or cranberries (halved if they are large)
½   teaspoon salt
Pepper to taste
Dash nutmeg

Macaroni and Cheese

The Riversong Lodge Cookbook ∽ KIRSTEN DIXON

1 onion, finely chopped
¼ cup unsalted butter
1 pound elbow macaroni
1 cup sour cream
½ cup crumbled feta cheese
¼ cup sliced Greek olives (about 15 olives)
Salt and freshly ground pepper to taste
1 cup spinach, cooked, drained, and chopped
½ cup chunky mild tomato salsa
½ cup shredded Parmesan cheese (optional)

We love to make macaroni and cheese in variations. It is nearly a universal food. This white and green version combines Greek olives, feta cheese, sour cream, salsa, and spinach.

• In a skillet, sauté the onion in butter until it is soft and golden. Cook the macaroni in the boiling salted water until tender. Drain.

• In a bowl, mix the hot macaroni, onion, sour cream, feta, and olives. Toss well and season to taste with salt and pepper. Add the spinach and toss again. Stir in the mild salsa. Sprinkle with Parmesan cheese, if desired. Serve warm.

MAKES 6 TO 8 SERVINGS.

Pecan Wild Rice

The Alaska Heritage Seafood Cookbook ∽
ANN CHANDONNET

3 cups water
½ cup raw wild rice, rinsed and drained
2 cups rich beef stock
(*continued* ➤)

Pecan Wild Rice is a savory side dish unique to Simon & Seafort's Bar and Grill in Anchorage, where it is dished up with fish entrées such as Cod Baked with Sun-Dried Tomato-Thyme Butter (**page 112**) and Rockfish with African Peanut Sauce (**page 114**). This is my own version, enhanced with tangerine rind.

• In a heavy saucepan, bring the 3 cups of water to a boil. Add the wild rice, reduce heat slightly, and cook at a gentle simmer, uncovered for 40 to 45 minutes or until rice is just tender. Drain. Keep warm.

• In another heavy saucepan, bring the beef stock to a boil. Add the white rice, reduce the heat slightly, cover, and simmer for another 15 minutes. Add the orange juice and stir. Cover and simmer for another 5 minutes, or until the rice is tender and the liquid has been absorbed. Stir in the tangerine rind.

• Heat the oil and butter in a frying pan over medium heat. Add the onion and sauté, stirring, for 5 to 7 minutes, or until wilted. Add the garlic for the final 2 minutes. Add the pecans and cook for 2 more minutes, stirring. Remove from heat.

• Combine the rices and the onion mixture. Season to taste with salt and pepper, fluffing the rice with a fork. Serve hot.

MAKES 6 SERVINGS.

Note: For the subtle Chinese fillip of tangerine rind, simply eat a tangerine 3 or 4 days ahead, saving the rind. Dry the rind at room temperature. Break the dried rind into little bits and fold into the rice.

1½ cups raw long-grain white rice
½ cup fresh orange juice
1 tablespoon finely chopped dried tangerine rind (**see Note**)
1 tablespoon olive oil
1 tablespoon butter
1 medium onion, coarsely chopped
1 clove fresh garlic, finely minced
½ cup coarsely chopped pecans
Salt and freshly ground black pepper, to taste

Skillet Garlic Potatoes

The Riversong Lodge Cookbook ∾ KIRSTEN DIXON

We serve these potatoes both as a breakfast dish and as a side dish for other meals. The longer the garlic cooks, the more it sweetens and mellows in flavor.

• Heat the olive oil in a large, heavy skillet over high heat. Spread the potatoes over the bottom of the pan and sauté for about 10 minutes. Turn the potatoes over and add the garlic. Continue to sauté until the potatoes are golden, about 10 minutes. Add the rosemary leaves, and season with salt and pepper to taste.

MAKES 6 SERVINGS.

¼ cup olive oil
1 pound potatoes, scrubbed and cut into cubes
10 cloves garlic, peeled and halved
Leaves from 1 large sprig fresh rosemary
Salt and freshly ground pepper to taste

Mushrooms and Sour Cream

Lowbush Moose ∽ GORDON NELSON

1 pound fresh
   mushrooms, sliced
¼ cup onion, minced
¼ cup butter
1 cup sour cream
2 tablespoons sherry
Salt and black pepper
   to taste

If there are any foods in the world that love each other more than sour cream and mushrooms, I haven't found them. Every time I drift home from the grocery store with a wistful look, my wife says, "Mushrooms and Sour Cream?"

• You can add this pair to just about anything and they will come up tasting wonderful. Try the basic recipe here and then try the suggested variations or dream up your own. Just think of me when you eat them and maybe some of that enjoyment will come my way through telepathy.

• Some additions you might wish to try on the second or third time: 1 clove of garlic, minced, added during the sautéing. A dash of nutmeg, 1 teaspoon of lemon juice, ½ teaspoon tarragon or dried parsley or fresh chives—any of these, or any combination, added with the seasoning.

• Sauté the mushrooms and onion in the butter for 5 minutes. Stir in the sour cream, sherry, and salt and pepper. Heat the mixture to a point just below boiling, but be careful not to let it boil.

• When this is hot you can serve it as a separate dish as is, or as a sauce on just about anything, although it goes especially well with rice, noodles, mashed potatoes, or broccoli.

MAKES 4 SERVINGS.

Seared Peppers and Onions with Molasses Balsamic Glaze

A Cache of Recipes ∽ LAURA COLE

½ large red onion
1 red bell pepper,
   seeded
   (*continued* ➤)

Serving these with our Grilled Marinated Flank Steak (page 155) complements their bold, savory flavor.

• Slice the onion in half, then into 6 long wedges. Slice each red, yellow, and green pepper into 8 long wedges.

• In a large, 2-inch-deep skillet, heat the olive oil over medium-high heat. Add the onion and sauté for 1 minute. Add the bell pepper wedges and sauté for 1 minute more. Add the molasses and balsamic vinegar, stirring to coat. When the peppers are tender, remove the pan from the heat. Season with salt, pepper, and thyme, and serve warm.

MAKES 4 SERVINGS.

1   yellow bell pepper, seeded
1   green bell pepper, seeded
1   tablespoon olive oil
2   tablespoons molasses
1   tablespoon balsamic vinegar
2   teaspoons kosher salt
2   teaspoons coarsely ground pepper
2   teaspoons chopped fresh thyme

Roasted Garlic Smashed Potatoes

A Cache of Recipes ∾ LAURA COLE

We refer to these as smashed potatoes because they are just coarsely mashed with the back of a spoon. Roasting the garlic gives it rich flavor and makes it easier to digest. Roasted garlic is a great food to have on hand. You can keep it refrigerated for up to two weeks.

• To make the roasted garlic: Preheat the oven to 350°F. Cut the tapered end off the head of garlic, very near the top, exposing the cloves. Drizzle the oil onto the cut end of the garlic, allowing it to seep in. Sprinkle the salt on top of the oil. Wrap the garlic tightly in foil and roast it for about 45 minutes. Test it by squeezing gently on the foil; the garlic should be very tender. Remove from the oven, and allow to cool before unwrapping the foil.

• To prepare the potatoes: In a small pan, over low heat, melt together the butter and cream; keep warm.

• Set the potatoes in a large pot, and add water to cover. Bring to a boil over medium-high heat. Boil the potatoes until tender, about 20 minutes. Insert a fork into the center of a potato to check doneness; the potato should easily fall off the fork. Quickly drain the potatoes and return them to the same pot. Add the warmed butter

Roasted Garlic
1   large head garlic
1   teaspoon olive oil
1   teaspoon kosher salt

Potatoes
4   tablespoons butter
¼   cup heavy cream
14 small red potatoes, washed
1   tablespoon salt
1   tablespoon freshly ground pepper

and cream. Smash the potatoes into the butter and cream with the back of a spoon. Unwrap the garlic and squeeze the roasted cloves out of their skins into the smashed potatoes. The roasted garlic should be fork tender. Continue mashing and smashing with the spoon. The potatoes should be slightly mashed, with larger chunks of potatoes and skin still visible. Season with salt and pepper.

MAKES 6 SERVINGS.

Cajun Rice

The Double Musky Inn Cookbook 〜
BOB AND DEANNA PERSONS

2 cups long-grain rice
2½ cups chicken stock
¼ cup diced green peppers
¼ cup diced white onions
¼ cup diced celery
2 tablespoons butter
1½ teaspoons granulated garlic
2¼ teaspoons salt

- Preheat oven to 500°F.
- Mix ingredients well and place in an oven-safe baking dish that's at least 2 inches higher than the rice mixture. Cover tightly with foil and bake 50 minutes. Remove the baking dish from the oven and pinch some rice between your fingers to make sure it's done. It should feel soft. The vegetables will be on the surface of the rice; stir them in. The rice can be left in a 150°F to 200°F oven for up to several hours if covered tightly. Put the rice into another dish for serving.

MAKES 4 TO 6 SERVINGS.

〜 *Note: This rice should be used the day you make it. It dries out quickly and cannot be stored successfully for serving again alone, but leftovers can be used as an ingredient in soup.*

Potato and Wild Mushroom Gratin

Wild Mushrooms ∾ CYNTHIA NIMS
(Northwest Homegrown Cookbook series)

The rich and creamy quality of a good potato gratin is deliciously embellished with wild mushrooms sandwiched between layers of thinly sliced potato. If you have a mandolin slicer, it's just the tool to make quick and easy work of slicing the potatoes uniformly. Any type of wild mushroom will be good for this recipe, a few different ones used together even better.

- Preheat the oven to 375°F. Generously butter a 12-inch oval gratin dish or other shallow 2-quart baking dish.

- Melt the butter in a large skillet over medium heat, add ¼ cup of the shallot and the garlic and sauté until tender and aromatic, 2 to 3 minutes. Add the mushrooms and sauté until they are tender and any liquid they release has evaporated, 10 to 12 minutes. Take the skillet from the heat and stir in the thyme with salt and pepper to taste. Set aside to cool.

- Peel the potatoes and cut them into ⅛-inch slices. Sprinkle about half of the remaining shallot over the bottom of the gratin dish and top with about one-third of the potato slices, slightly overlapping in an even layer. Season the potatoes with salt and pepper. Top with half of the mushroom mixture, spreading it out evenly, and sprinkle with one-third of the Parmesan cheese. Top with another third of the potato slices, the remaining mushrooms, and another third of the Parmesan cheese. Finish with the remaining potatoes, arranging the slices in an attractive pattern.

- Stir together the cream and half-and-half in a small bowl, then pour the cream mixture evenly over the potatoes. Sprinkle the remaining shallot and cheese over, seasoning once again with salt and pepper. Set the baking dish on a rimmed baking sheet to catch any drips, and bake until the edges of the gratin are bubbling and the potatoes are quite tender (pierce through the layers with a small knife to check), about 1 hour 15 minutes. If the top is well browned before the potatoes are tender, top the gratin loosely with a piece of buttered foil. Let sit for a few minutes before scooping out to serve.

MAKES 6 TO 8 SERVINGS.

3 tablespoons unsalted butter
½ cup minced shallot or onion
1 teaspoon minced garlic
1 pound wild mushrooms, brushed clean, trimmed, and thinly sliced
1 teaspoon minced thyme
Salt and freshly ground black pepper
2 pounds russet potatoes
¾ cup grated Parmesan cheese
1 cup whipping cream
1 cup half-and-half

Chickweed Oriental

Discovering Wild Plants ～ JANICE J. SCHOFIELD

2   cups chickweed tips,
    snipped fine with
    scissors
1   cup cleaned
    fiddleheads
¼   cup chopped
    dandelion greens
2   tablespoons chopped
    sorrel
1   tablespoon grated
    gingerroot
2   tablespoons sesame
    oil
½   cup pineapple chunks
1   tablespoon soy sauce
12 ounces (1 package)
    chow mein noodles

• Sauté greens and gingerroot in hot oil for 3 to 5 minutes. Add pineapple chunks and soy sauce. Heat briefly. Serve immediately on chow mein noodles.

MAKES 2 SERVINGS.

Knik Skillet Greens

Tired Wolf ～ GORDON NELSON

1   tablespoon butter
1   tablespoon vegetable
    oil
1   onion, sliced,
    separated into rings
1   green pepper
    (optional)
1   pound shredded
    garden greens—
    (*continued* ➤)

During the summer months, our family enjoys the wealth of greens our garden provides. The favorite is Swiss chard, but if it's green and tasty, we'll cook it. Try this recipe with what you have to cook.

• In your large skillet over medium heat, melt the butter and add the vegetable oil. Sauté the onion and green pepper about 5 minutes, until tender but crisp.

• Add the greens, salt, and pepper to the skillet and cover. Simmer 5 to 10 minutes, until the greens are tender.

• Or try this recipe in a microwave oven. With the oven set on high, cook the onion and pepper in a microwave-safe 3-quart container for 3 minutes, or until vegetables are crisp-tender. Add the greens and cook 2 minutes. Stir well, cook another 2 minutes, season as above and serve at once.

chard, spinach, beet, or turnip tops or even the lettuces (8 packed cups)
1 teaspoon salt
¼ teaspoon pepper

MAKES 4 SERVINGS.

Cranberry Stuffing

Alaska Wild Berry Guide and Cookbook ⌒

• Run the cranberries through a food chopper and add the sugar. Cook celery, parsley, and diced ham in butter for 5 minutes. Add the bread crumbs, seasoning, and berries and blend lightly. This is particularly good with baked moose heart, wild duck, or poultry.

MAKES 8 SERVINGS.

1 cup lowbush cranberries
¼ cup sugar
¼ cup chopped celery
2 tablespoons chopped parsley
½ cup diced ham or bacon
4 tablespoons butter or margarine
3 cups stale bread crumbs
1 cup cornbread crumbs
Poultry seasonings to taste

Cajun Sausage Dressing

The Double Musky Inn Cookbook ⌒
BOB AND DEANNA PERSONS

• Preheat oven to 425°F degrees.
• Finely shred day-old bread into crumbs, using a food processor or grater; the bread should not be too dry or stale.

1 loaf day-old bread
(*continued* ➤)

1 tablespoon diced
jalapeños
2½ cups diced celery
2½ cups sliced
green onions
1½ cups diced green
peppers
2 hot link sausages,
about 4 ounces each,
peeled and diced
2 tablespoons
Worcestershire sauce
4 tablespoons
butter/margarine
blend, melted

Measure out 5 cups of bread crumbs. Add 1 tablespoon of diced jalapeños.

• Mix all of the ingredients together in a large bowl. Put the dressing mixture in a deep baking dish, spread it level, and cover it tightly with foil.

• Bake the dressing for 30 minutes, remove from oven, and stir it well. Cover and re-place the dressing in the oven for 30 minutes more. Remove the dressing from the oven again, stir, and put it back in the oven, uncovered this time, for 20 more minutes or until the top is slightly browned.

MAKES 4 TO 6 SERVINGS.

∾ *Note: The cooking time for this dressing can vary considerably depending on the oven and the dish it is cooked in.*

Greens Supreme

Discovering Wild Plants ∾ JANICE J. SCHOFIELD
Recipe by Mairiis Davidson-Hollister, Homer

4 cups fresh nettles,
chopped
Boiling water
½ cup grated Parmesan
cheese

• Place nettles in steamer basket over boiling water. Cook 3 to 5 minutes. Top nettles with Parmesan cheese and serve immediately.

MAKES 2 SERVINGS.

Matanuska Pickled Carrots

Hibrow Cow ∾ GORDON NELSON

3 tablespoons veg-
etable oil
1 teaspoon salt
(*continued* ➤)

Another vegetable that grows well in the Matanuska Valley is the carrot. Naturally after you have served them boiled, stewed, sliced, and grated, and added them to every dish you make, there will be some left. I had all I needed in the freezer and still had carrots left in the garden. Any suggestion would have been considered. Into this void of ideas came this recipe from a friend. This dish is reported to keep for a week, but in my experience it is gone within two days.

- In a saucepan over medium heat combine 2 tablespoons oil, 1 teaspoon salt, and 1 teaspoon sugar. Add carrots, green peppers, celery, and water. Bring to a boil, reduce heat and simmer uncovered. Stir occasionally during the 5 to 10 minutes necessary for vegetables to become tender. Remove from heat.

- In a second saucepan, sauté onions in 1 tablespoon oil and ¼ teaspoon sugar until transparent. Add onions to carrot mixture and mix well. Add catsup and lemon juice and mix one more time.

- Transfer carrots to a covered bowl and chill in the refrigerator. Serve cold as a salad, or as a garnish for fish dishes, or add some to your favorite sandwich. And finish the bowl as a midnight snack.

1¼ teaspoons sugar
2 cups peeled or scraped, shredded carrots
1 cup thinly sliced green peppers
⅓ cup finely chopped celery
¼ cup water
1 cup finely chopped onions
¼ cup tomato catsup
2 tablespoons lemon juice

MAKES 4 SERVINGS.

....

Fiddlehead Ferns and Garlic

The Winterlake Lodge Cookbook ∼ KIRSTEN DIXON

The first time I ate fiddlehead ferns, I tried them fresh off the fern, and I got a terrible stomachache. Don't eat them without blanching them first, which neutralizes the enzymes that can upset the stomach. Fiddleheads are best when picked still tightly curled. Peel off the papery skin and trim any remaining stalk. A handful is about right for a reasonable serving. Fiddleheads are abundant in Alaska. They are a warm, welcome reminder that spring is here.

- In a large sauté pan, melt the butter over medium heat. Add the garlic and sauté until it is aromatic but not browned, about 2 minutes. Add the fiddleheads and sauté for 1 to 2 minutes. Add the chicken broth and cover the pan with a lid or with aluminum foil to allow the ferns to steam slightly, cooking for 5 minutes. Sprinkle the fiddleheads with parsley. Season the fiddleheads with salt and pepper to taste.

½ cup butter
2 cloves garlic, peeled and minced
1 pound fiddlehead ferns, trimmed and cleaned
¼ cup chicken broth
2 tablespoons Italian parsley
Salt and freshly ground Winterlake Pepper Blend (page 59)

MAKES 4 SERVINGS.

Fairbanks garden party.

Alaska Cranberry Tea

Alaska Wild Berry Guide and Cookbook
RECIPE BY RACHEL ADKINS, NORTH POLE

• Cook cranberries, cinnamon sticks, and water until berries are tender. Strain. Add lemon, orange juice, and sugar. Heat until sugar is dissolved. Serve hot.

1	quart lowbush cranberries
2	cinnamon sticks
3	quarts water
6	tablespoons lemon juice
2	cups orange juice
2	cups sugar

Rose Hip Juice

Alaska Wild Berry Guide and Cookbook

If possible, gather your rose hips before the first frost.
• Clean and remove the tails. Place the hips in a kettle with enough water to completely cover the fruit. Bring to a boil slowly, reduce the heat, and simmer for 15 minutes, or until the fruit is soft. Strain the hips through a wet jelly bag overnight. Pour the extracted juice into a container you can cover, then store it in the refrigerator, where it will keep for several weeks—ideal for having on hand throughout the preserving season.

Rose hips
Water

Highbush Cranberry Rhubarb Ade

Cooking Alaskan ∿
Recipe adapted from *An Alaskan Cook Book*

2 cups highbush
   cranberry juice
2 cups rhubarb juice
2 cups water
1½ cups sugar

Simmer juices and water. Add sugar and simmer until dissolved. Chill before serving. Or, pasteurize to boiling point, pour into sterilized jars, seal and process in boiling water bath for 15 minutes. This cranberry-rhubarb juice is also good mixed half and half with a carbonated beverage of your choice, such as lemon-lime soda.

Carl Berlin's Clover Wine

The Riversong Lodge Cookbook ∿ KIRSTEN DIXON

1 gallon clover blos-
   soms
1 gallon boiling water
3 pounds sugar
3 oranges, washed
   and sliced
3 lemons, washed
   and sliced
2 packages
   (2 tablespoons)
   active dry yeast

I'm not sure whether Carl Berlin is the man who sent me this recipe, or just an early owner of the recipe card. Regardless, the faded 3-by-5-inch card is a treasure in my recipe box. Remember that this is an old recipe—wine-making techniques have become more sophisticated over the years. If you've never made wine before, I recommend that you check with a local home-brewing supplier before attempting this recipe.

• Place the clover blossoms in a large, spotlessly clean container (it must be free of bacteria). Pour boiling water over blossoms. Loosely cover and let stand for 3 days.

• Strain the liquid, discarding the blossoms, and add the sugar, oranges, lemons, and yeast. Place the liquid in a glass or ceramic container and let it ferment at room temperature for 3 weeks. Cover the top with cheesecloth, but do not seal the container or it may explode.

• Strain the liquid and pour into clean, sterilized bottles. Cap or cork the wine.

MAKES 1 GALLON.

Berry Lemonade

The Winterlake Lodge Cookbook ∿ KIRSTEN DIXON

This easy but beautiful summertime lemonade has a little fizz to it. I buy pure raspberry juice concentrate in the health food section of the supermarket. Lemons are expensive in Alaska, so fresh lemonade is especially valued.

- In a large pitcher, combine the sparkling water, sugar, and lemon juice. Stir well to dissolve the sugar. Chill.
- Stir in the fruit juice concentrate. Pour the lemonade into tall glasses and add ice cubes. Place fresh raspberries on top of the ice cubes.

MAKES 4 TO 6 SERVINGS.

4 cups sparkling water
2 cups sugar
2 cups freshly squeezed lemon juice
2 teaspoons raspberry juice concentrate
¼ cup red raspberries

Dandelion Cocktail

Discovering Wild Plants ∿ JANICE J. SCHOFIELD

Place all ingredients in a blender; blend for 3 to 5 minutes.

MAKES 3 SERVINGS.

100 small, washed dandelion leaves
1½ cups tomato juice
2 tablespoons Worcesterhire sauce
Dash of Tabasco®

Hot Cranberry Cider

The Winterlake Lodge Cookbook ⌒ KIRSTEN DIXON

4 cups apple cider
4 cups cranberry juice
2 1-inch cinnamon
   sticks
2 1-inch strips of
   orange peel
1 cardamom pod,
   crushed

At Winterlake, we make this aromatic drink in a large pot and set it on the woodstove to keep warm for guests who come in from dog mushing or skiing. It is enticing and delicious. To make this drink into a toddy, add a jigger of rum and a tablespoon of butter to each mug.

• In a stainless steel or enamel saucepan, combine the apple cider and the cranberry juice. Into a small piece of 100 percent cotton cheesecloth, put the cinnamon sticks, orange peel, and cardamom pod. Tie the cloth securely. Drop the spice packet into the liquid and bring the mixture to a boil; simmer for 10 minutes. Remove the pan from heat, remove the spice packet, and serve.

MAKES 8 CUPS.

▶ MRS. WAGNER IN
HER GARDEN PATCH.

Alaska strawberry blossoms.

Rose Hip Jelly

Alaska Wild Berry Guide and Cookbook

Place rose hips in a pan with the water. Boil until the hips are soft. Put through a coarse sieve and drain through a jelly bag. Measure the juice into a saucepan and add the lemon juice. Add ¾ as much sugar as you have juice. Boil rapidly for 10 minutes and test for the jelly stage. If the test is negative, continue cooking the juice until it jells. Pour into hot, sterilized jelly glasses and seal at once with paraffin and lids.

2 cups cleaned and seeded rose hips

2 cups water

4 tablespoons lemon juice

Sugar

The Sheet Test for Jelly: If you do not have a jelly thermometer to tell you when the boiling juice has reached the jelly stage, use the "sheet" test instead. Dip a cold metal spoon into the boiling liquid and then hold it from 12 to 18 inches above the pan but out of the path of rising steam. Turn the spoon so the jelly runs off the edge. If 2 or more drops form and run together before dripping off the edge of the spoon as separate drops, the jelly stage has been reached. It usually takes from 8 to 15 minutes to reach the sheet or jelly stage.

Cranberry Luscious

Alaska Wild Berry Guide and Cookbook ⌇

2　cups currants
4　cups lowbush
　　cranberries
2　cups strawberries
2　cups raspberries
2　cups blueberries
Sugar

- Clean the currants, but don't remove the stems. Clean and stem the other berries. Place currants into kettle and crush enough to start the juice. Cook the currants, stirring and mashing all the while, until they appear whitish. Strain through a jelly bag and add 1 cup sugar for each cup juice to make currant syrup.
- In a separate container, combine all uncooked berries and weigh. Add as much sugar as there is uncooked fruit by weight. Pour currant syrup over the fresh fruit mixture and let stand overnight. Next day bring the mixture to a boil for 15 minutes, then set aside in a cool place for 48 hours, allowing the berries to absorb the syrup and become plump.
- Heat again, then pour into hot, sterilized canning jars and seal with lids. Process for 15 minutes in boiling water bath.

2　oranges
1　lemon
⅛　teaspoon baking soda
1¾　cups water
4　cups lowbush
　　cranberries
6½　cups sugar
3　ounces liquid pectin

Lowbush Cranberry Marmalade

Alaska Wild Berry Guide and Cookbook ⌇

- Remove seeds from the oranges and lemon and cut fruit into large pieces. Do not remove peels. Grind fruit. Add the baking soda and water; cover and simmer for 20 minutes, stirring occasionally. Add berries and continue simmering, covered, for another 10 minutes. Measure exactly 5 cups of the prepared fruit into a large saucepan and add the sugar. Bring to a full, rolling boil for 1 minute. Remove from heat and stir in the pectin at once. Skim and stir for about 5 minutes, allowing the marmalade to cool slightly. Ladle into hot, sterilized canning jars and seal with lids. Process for 15 minutes in a boiling water bath.

Rhubarb Strawberry Jelly

Cooking Alaskan ⤳ Recipe adapted from *Rhubarb Recipes*

• Crush strawberries, add to rhubarb, and bring to a boil. Strain juice through a jelly bag. Use 3½ cups juice. Combine with sugar and bring to a boil. Add 1 bottle pectin and boil 1 minute. Remove from heat and skim. Pour into jelly glasses and pour on a ⅛-inch layer of paraffin. Yields 6 to 7 half-pints.

1	quart of rhubarb, cut very fine
2	quarts ripe strawberries
6	cups sugar
6	ounces pectin

Short-Cooked Berry Jam

Cooking Alaskan ⤳
Recipe adapted from *Collecting and Using Alaska's Wild Berries*

• Measure crushed berries into a large kettle. Add sugar and stir until dissolved. Place on high heat, stirring constantly until it comes to a full boil. Boil hard 1 minute, stirring constantly. Remove from heat; at once stir in liquid pectin. Skim off foam with metal spoon. Then stir and skim for five minutes to cool slightly. Pour into hot sterilized jars. Add lids. Process for 15 minutes in boiling water bath. Makes 3 to 4 pints.

6	cups crushed berries
8½	cups sugar
3	ounces liquid pectin

Homemade Fresh Blueberry Jam

The Winterlake Lodge Cookbook ⤳ KIRSTEN DIXON

Sometimes I add a bit of lemon and a clove to this recipe.
• Into an enamel or stainless steel medium saucepan, combine the blueberries and sugar. Lightly mash the berries if you prefer. Bring the mixture to a boil over high heat. Reduce the heat to medium-high and gently boil for 15 to 20 minutes.

4	cups wild blueberries
4	cups sugar

MAKES 4 CUPS.

Sitka Rose Honey

Alaska Sourdough ⌒ RUTH ALLMAN

5 pounds sugar
6 cups water
1 lump of alum the size of a cherry
24 Sitka wild rose blossoms (or 8 double rose blossoms)
24 white clover blossoms
12 red clover blossoms

Honey without the aid of the bees!

• Boil sugar and water to 232°F. Then add alum. Boil 4 minutes. Remove from heat.

• Add the blossoms. Stir well until blossoms all wilted. Let stand 10 minutes; stir frequently. Strain. If you wish to tint to a light pink, add food coloring with a petal. Seal while hot in half-pint jars.

Riversong Red Pepper Relish

The Riversong Lodge Cookbook ⌒ KIRSTEN DIXON

4 cups red bell peppers, halved, seeded, deveined, and minced
2 cups minced red onion
2 cups red wine vinegar
1 small Thai or other hot pepper, seeded and minced
1 tablespoon minced fresh ginger
1 cup honey
1½ cups light brown sugar

This is the condiment that I couldn't face winter without. Try it on stew, burgers, grilled fish, or pasta.

• Combine all the ingredients except the honey and sugar in a large saucepan. Bring the mixture to a boil over medium heat. Reduce the heat and simmer until the peppers and onions are soft, about 10 minutes. Add the honey and sugar.

• Continue to simmer, stirring often, until the peppers and onions are translucent and the mixture is thick, about 30 minutes. Ladle the relish into hot, sterilized half-pint jars, leaving ¼-inch headspace. Adjust the lids and process in a boiling-water bath for 10 minutes.

MAKES 5 CUPS.

Juneau Salmon Bake BBQ Sauce

Life's a Fish and Then You Fry ∾ RANDY BAYLISS

The Juneau Salmon Bake Barbecue Sauce remains my favorite. And it's as simple as it is excellent.

- Add 1 cup of brown sugar to a melted stick of butter and the juice of half a lemon. Dredge the salmon fillets in oil before putting them on the grill, skin side down at first. Baste both sides with the sauce, turning frequently. You'll use this one a lot.

MAKES 1½ CUPS.

Ginger Dipping Sauce for Steamed Crab

Life's a Fish and Then You Fry ∾ RANDY BAYLISS

The Chinese consider the "coolest" of seafood to be crab and thus often serve crab with ginger. The following recipe best demonstrates the Oriental principle of harmony of tastes. The dipping sauce can also be served with shrimp and tempura.

- Mix the sauce ingredients together and simmer for a few minutes. Cool slightly before serving with the crab.

MAKES 4 SERVINGS.

∾ *Note: This same ginger dipping sauce can serve as both marinade and glaze for barbecued fish. For a marinade, simply dilute the sauce with an equal amount of water. For a glaze, take a cup of the dipping sauce and simmer it in a saucepan. In a bowl, dissolve 1 ounce of cornstarch solution to the sauce until it thickens, stirring constantly. Marinate the fish for at least a ½ hour. Once on the grill, brush the glaze on the fish.*

1 ounce grated (pulverized) ginger
2 ounces soy sauce
2 ounces rice vinegar (substitute mild white vinegar)
1 ounce honey
Steamed crab for 4 servings, not overcooked

Clarified Butter

The Alaska Heritage Seafood Cookbook ～
ANN CHANDONNET

1 cup unsalted butter

Many chefs are trained to use clarified butter when cooking because it has a higher scorching point than whole butter. Clarified butter is the clear yellow liquid that separates from the milk solids when melted butter cools. Known to Yankee cooks as drawn butter, it is also served as a dipping sauce for steamed shellfish.

●In a heavy saucepan, melt the butter over medium-high heat. Skim off any foam that rises to the surface of the butter. Remove from the heat and allow the butter to cool.

●When cool, drain off the clear liquid at the top; this is the clarified butter. Discard the milk solids at the bottom of the pan. Keep the clarified butter in a covered glass jar in the refrigerator. It can be prepped several weeks in advance.

MAKES ABOUT ⅔ CUP.

Pesto Sauce

Life's a Fish and Then You Fry ～ RANDY BAYLISS

2 ounces olive oil
1 cup fresh basil leaves
3 cloves garlic
1 ounce pine nuts
2 ounces Parmesan
    cheese

Pesto has been called the poetry of the fields, combining the fragrances of the Mediterranean. Basically, pesto uses basil, olive oil, cheese, and garlic. Purists claim that pesto must use the Italian basil grown near Genoa, which must be ground by hand in special marble mortars. Traditionalists serve pesto with fettuccine and sliced, boiled potatoes. This recipe requires a food processor instead of a mortar.

●Blend all ingredients in a food processor. If the pesto is to be frozen, leave out the cheese until the sauce is thawed for use. Pesto can be blended into mayonnaise or incorporated as part of homemade mayonnaise. Serve Pesto Mayonnaise with poached fish and boiled potatoes.

Apple Cherry Chutney

The Winterlake Lodge Cookbook ∿ KIRSTEN DIXON

This recipe will fill your kitchen with the delicious sweet-sour aroma of cherries and vinegar. You may always add more cherries, less apples, or more onions to create your own version. To make this chutney spicier, you may add minced spicy pepper or some pepper flakes. This chutney is an attractive and tasty accompaniment for salmon, especially our salmon burgers. It is delicious dolloped onto a toast point covered with melted cheese as well. Frozen cherries will work just as well as fresh. Serve this colorful chutney with your favorite dish, or make large batches and preserve the chutney in glass jars.

• Heat the oil in medium saucepan over medium-high heat. Add in the onions and reduce the heat to low, pressing down a sheet of aluminum foil over the onions and then covering the saucepan with a lid. This allows the onions to remain tender and moist while cooking. Simmer the onions for about 10 minutes or until they are softened. Remove the lid and the foil and add the vinegar, apples, cherries, ginger, and allspice. Stir the mixture and allow the chutney to simmer for about 25 minutes.

2 tablespoons light olive oil
2 medium red onions, thinly sliced
1 cup cider vinegar
2 large tart, green apples (such as Granny Smith), peeled, cored, and diced
1 cup cherries, pitted and sliced
½-inch knob of fresh ginger, peeled and minced
½ teaspoon ground allspice

MAKES 3 CUPS.

That fall we picked forty gallons of blueberries and preserved them with layers of sugar in wooden kegs. We picked another ten gallons of low-bush cranberries for preserves, plus an assortment of other varieties. We picked and dried a large supply of mushrooms. In late fall, we were still catching a few pike, whitefish, and worn-out salmon in the gill nets set in back eddies along the Koyukuk River. We split and hung these fish to dry, since besides being excellent dog food, they made good bait for marten and mink sets.

—*Shadows on the Koyukuk,* SIDNEY HUNTINGTON WITH JIM REARDEN

Cranberry Chutney

The Winterlake Lodge Cookbook ⮑ KIRSTEN DIXON

1 tablespoon light
  olive oil
1 small red onion,
  finely chopped
1 (12-ounce) bag fresh
  or frozen whole
  cranberries
⅔ cup sugar
3 tablespoons
  cider vinegar
1 clove garlic, peeled
  and minced
¼-inch knob of fresh
  ginger, peeled and
  minced
½ teaspoon salt
⅛ teaspoon red
  pepper flakes

Cranberries come in high-bush and low-bush varieties in Alaska, and they are both good. This recipe uses the big commercial cranberries found in the market, but use wild Alaskan berries if you can get them.

● Heat the oil in a 3-quart heavy saucepan over medium heat. Add the red onion, stirring occasionally, until softened, about 3 minutes. Stir in the cranberries, sugar, cider vinegar, garlic, ginger, salt, and red pepper flakes. Simmer the mixture, uncovered, stirring occasionally, just until the berries pop, about 10 to 12 minutes. Can the chutney or store it covered in the refrigerator for about 1 week.

MAKES ABOUT 2 CUPS.

I thawed a bowl of blueberries, bruised them up a bit for more juice, added some white sugar and syrup, and enjoyed a treat to celebrate the return of the sun.

—*One Man's Wilderness*, SAM KEITH FROM THE JOURNALS AND PHOTOGRAPHS OF RICHARD PROENNEKE

Apricot Kiwi Salsa

The Alaska Heritage Seafood Cookbook ⮑
ANN CHANDONNET

4 apricots cleaned,
  seeded, and diced
  (*continued* ➜)

This speedy salsa is delectable with grilled salmon. It suavely combines fruits and vegetables with hot peppers for a palate-tingling side dish—the modern equivalent of the colonial "relish." The recipe originated with the Providence Nutrition Center, Anchorage.

• Prepare apricots, kiwifruit, tomatoes, green onions, peppers, and basil leaves. Dissolve sugar in lime juice and vinegar. Toss all ingredients together in a nonreactive container. Serve at once.

MAKES ABOUT 2 CUPS.

Note: Wear gloves or oil hands well when preparing the pepperoncini peppers, and avoid touching your eyes. Discard seeds.

2 kiwifruit, peeled and sliced

6 cherry tomatoes, seeded and julienned

½ bunch green onions, finely sliced

2 pepperoncini peppers, seeded and finely sliced (see Note)

6 fresh basil leaves, julienned

2 teaspoons sugar

Juice of ½ lime

¼ cup red wine vinegar

Fresh Fruit Salsa for Salmon

A Cache of Recipes ⚬ LAURA COLE

The bold flavors of the mango and lime in this salsa pair wonderfully with the rich, smoky flavor of grilled salmon. You can use different fruit in this recipe to suit your taste, but always use the freshest and ripest fruit available. Make this salsa the day you plan to serve it.

• In a large bowl, mix all of the ingredients together. Cover and refrigerate for 2 to 4 hours. Allow the salsa to come to room temperature before serving. Mix it together again just before serving.

MAKES 2 CUPS.

1 mango, peeled and diced

2 kiwifruit, peeled and diced

⅓ cup diced cantaloupe

4 large strawberries, hulled and diced

⅓ cup diced red onion

2 tablespoons fresh lime juice

2 teaspoons minced jalapeño chile

1 teaspoon kosher salt

½ cup chopped fresh cilantro

Cranberry Relish

Discovering Wild Plants ∿ JANICE J. SCHOFIELD

2 cups cranberries
1 orange, peeled
1 cup pineapple
1 cup cleaned
    rose hips
½ cup walnuts
½ cup honey
2 tablespoons
    lemon juice

● In a food grinder with medium blade, grind cranberries, orange, pineapple, rose hips, and walnuts. Add honey and lemon juice. Mix well. Let stand 24 hours to blend flavors.

MAKES 4 TO 6 SERVINGS.

Homemade Zucchini Relish

The Winterlake Lodge Cookbook ∿ KIRSTEN DIXON

2 medium zucchini,
    finely chopped
1 medium red onion,
    finely chopped
1 red bell pepper, finely
    chopped
1 green bell pepper,
    finely chopped
2 tablespoons salt
1 cup sugar
1 cup cider vinegar
½ teaspoon celery seed
½ teaspoon ground
    turmeric

Every Alaskan gardener looks for clever zucchini recipes because zucchini grows so well in the Northland. This tasty relish is a Winterlake favorite served at lunchtime alongside big hamburgers and homemade buns. Soaking the vegetables hydrates them before putting them into the pickling solution.

● In a large bowl combine the zucchini, onion, red bell pepper, green bell pepper, and salt. Toss the mixture, then cover it with cold water. Let the mixture soak for about 1 hour. Drain the vegetables and rinse.

● In a medium saucepan, place the vegetables, and add the sugar, vinegar, celery seed, and turmeric and combine. Cover and simmer gently for 10 minutes.

MAKES 2 PINTS.

Highbush Cranberry Catsup

Alaska Wild Berry Guide and Cookbook

● Cook berries and onions in the water until soft. Put through a sieve and return the pulp to large cooking pot. Add remaining ingredients. Bring to a boil, reduce heat, and cook until thick and catsup-like in consistency. Stir frequently to keep from sticking. Pour into sterilized canning jars and seal immediately. Process for 5 to 10 minutes in a boiling water bath. Use Highbush Cranberry Catsup just like a regular tomato catsup.

Note: Highbush cranberries are best when picked slightly underripe, for they become bitter as they ripen.

6	pounds highbush cranberries
1¼	pounds sweet white onions
3	cups water
3	cups mild vinegar
6	cups sugar
1	tablespoon cloves
1	tablespoon cinnamon
1	tablespoon allspice
1	tablespoon salt
2	tablespoons celery salt
1½	teaspoons pepper

In 34 years of life, I have never been this organized. At this moment, I know what I will eat every day for the next 17 weeks. Foil packs of freeze-dried dinners, gorp bags the size of basketballs, a dozen boxes of pilot bread, 17 jars of peanut butter, 11 spears of pepperoni and other future meals coat the ground floor of Smit's home. Now comes the hard part: measuring cups of raisins, oatmeal, Cream of Wheat, gorp, refried beans. Sorting candy bars, vitamin C tablets, rations of toilet paper. Ciphering how many of these items I'll need for a six-day stretch, or an eight-day stretch. Placing the items in 17 cardboard boxes that will remain in Smit's house until some-one delivers them to me.

—Walking My Dog, Jane, NED ROZELL

Petersburg Tartar Sauce

Hibrow Cow ⮴ GORDON NELSON

½ cup mayonnaise
½ cup sour cream
¼ cup minced
 green onions
¼ cup finely chopped
 dill pickles
1 tablespoon drained
 and mashed capers

Way back in my youth, when I lived in Petersburg, it was known as the Halibut Capital of the World. It was a natural to have a tartar sauce named after it. So when this recipe came my way, I remembered.

• Combine all ingredients in a small bowl. Mix well. Cover and chill until used. Can be thinned with a little milk if it seems thick for your taste. Serves four nicely. Try it on any fish, crab, or other seafood.

SERVES 4.

Fresh Raspberry Sauce

Baked Alaska ⮴ SARAH EPPENBACH

2 cups raspberries
3 tablespoons sugar,
 more to taste
1 tablespoon lemon
 juice, more to taste
1 to 2 tablespoons kirsch,
 Cognac, or orange-
 flavored liqueur
 (optional)

Among the most useful and beautiful of dessert sauces, Fresh Raspberry Sauce provides a finishing touch to cakes, ice creams, or fresh fruit. You can substitute strawberries for all or part of the raspberries.

• Sieve the berries to remove the seeds, and transfer the puree to an electric blender. Add the sugar and lemon juice and blend at medium-high speed for 30 seconds. Taste, adding additional lemon juice and sugar as needed. Blend in the optional liqueur and refrigerate until serving.

MAKES ABOUT 1½ CUPS.

Sources

The sources for the recipes in this cookbook are cookbooks and other books published by Alaska Northwest Books over more than 40 years, starting with the press's first cookbook, *The Alaska Camp Cook*, released in 1963. The other books, which yielded the book's sidebars, include intriguing insights into the culture of food in Alaska.

Cookbooks

The Alaskan Camp Cook: Trail-Tested Recipes from the Kitchens and Campfires of Alaskan Big Game Guides, 1963. The first cookbook published by Alaska Northwest Books, this unique collection offers recipes that were contributed by big game guides, their wives, and other Alaska sportsmen. Included is no-nonsense advice on how to dress or clean and deftly prepare the Last Frontier's natural bounty, from ptarmigan and Dall sheep to shellfish and wild berries. With early illustrations by Rie Muñoz.

The Alaska Wild Berry Guide and Cookbook, 1982. An illustrated field guide and a cookbook . . . it's a unique combination, and the perfect way to collect all the facts about the nearly 50 berries indigenous to Alaska. Complete field information is provided—where to find the berries, what they are, how to recognize them— plus over 270 delicious recipes for cooking them. Everything from desserts to jams, beverages, candies, trail food, even wines. Compiled by the editors of *Alaska* magazine.

Allman, Ruth. *Alaska Sourdough*, 1976. In this classic last word on sourdough cookery, there are recipes for Alaska frontier staples, such as Basic Sourdough Starter, Sourdough Bread, and Sourdough Hotcakes, with time-tested advice and lore. Author Ruth Allman, raised by Alaska pioneers Judge and Mrs. James Wickersham, established the remote Tongass Lodge with her husband, Jack, where she developed many of her sourdough recipes. In later years, as hostess and caretaker of the House of Wickersham, the judge's home in Juneau, she often served tourists her Flaming Sourdough Waffles.

Bayliss, Randy. *Life's a Fish and Then You Fry: An Alaska Seafood Cookbook*, 2002. Seafood that's quick, simple, and delicious—those are the watchwords for Randy Bayliss, a Juneau mariner and veteran cooking columnist. The volume holds more than 200 distinctive recipes for entrees, soups, and salads featuring Alaska seafood. But it's more than your standard cookbook. Packed with the visual escapades of Ray Troll's fishy art, this entertaining book is about good food served with good humor and a dollop of sensual double entendre.

Chandonnet, Ann. *The Alaska Heritage Seafood Cookbook: Great Recipes from Alaska's Rich Kettle of Fish*, 1995. This hearty cookbook pays tribute to one of Alaska's greatest resources. Full of cooking tips and Alaska lore, the collection offers traditional and contemporary recipes such as Macadamia Nut–Crusted Halibut, Mrs. Gruening's Crab Bisque, and Rockfish with African Peanut Sauce.

Cole, Laura. *A Cache of Recipes: From the Kitchens of Camp Denali and North Face Lodge*, 2002. In this collection, chef Laura Cole shares favorite recipes for healthy, delectable food that she prepares for the guests at Camp Denali and North Face Lodge. Travelers can enjoy spectacular views of Mount McKinley and the Alaska Range while savoring such delicious fare as Swedish Oven Pancakes, Apricot-Glazed Pork Tenderloin, Vegetarian Lasagna, and Pumpkin Torte.

Cooking Alaskan, 1983. This classic collection of Alaskan recipes by Alaskans was created by the editors of Alaska Northwest Books. It is a whopping book filled with loads of how-to information (how to smoke fish, how to cook a walrus) and recipes for over 1,400 Northland favorites from Venison Jerky and Alaska King Crab Chowder to Sourdough Honey Biscuits and Alaskan Blueberry Pie.

Dixon, Kirsten. *The Riversong Lodge Cookbook: World-Class Cooking in the Alaskan Bush*, 1993. "No roads lead to the Riversong Lodge kitchen." Thus starts chef Kirsten Dixon's distinctive, personal cookbook, which is a delicious mix of recipes and vignettes from one of Alaska's internationally famous wilderness lodges. Enjoy Riversong Moose Stew, Broiled Salmon in a Horseradish Ginger Crust, and Sourdough Bread Pudding with Yukon Jack Sauce. With an abundance of spectacular photographs by Fred Hirschmann.

————. *The Winterlake Lodge Cookbook: Culinary Adventures in the Wilderness*, 2003. Chef Kirsten Dixon, hostess at Winterlake Lodge, one of Alaska's rustic fishing resorts, offers 100 delicious recipes that pay tribute to Alaska's seasonal bounty. Between accounts of adventure-filled days at the lodge, Kirsten serves up such tempting delights as Alaska Salmon Burgers with Apple Cherry Chutney, Pan-Seared Duck with Blueberry Sauce, Fiddlehead Ferns and Garlic, and Cardamom Carrot Cake.

Eppenbach, Sarah. *Baked Alaska: Recipes for Sweet Comforts from the North Country*, 1997. This charmingly illustrated book contains over 70 delicious recipes for sweet treats from Alaska's kitchens. From tea breads to muffins, custards to cobblers, it is a scrumptious sampling of baked goods Alaskans cherish. How about Lemon Raspberry Muffins, Rie's Dutch Honey Cake, or Clinkerdagger's Burnt Cream?

Guild, Ben. *The Alaskan Mushroom Hunter's Guide*, 1977. This fully illustrated book is the complete guide to Alaska's mushrooms for the amateur mushroom collector. Published 40 years ago, it remains the first and only full treatment of Alaska's mushrooms. An unexpected plus is the collection of yummy recipes for wild mushrooms at the back of the book.

Nelson, Gordon R. *Lowbush Moose, and Other Alaskan Recipes*, 1978. A lifetime Alaskan and retired Alaska State Trooper, Gordon Nelson gathered this collection of recipes from his multifarious life experiences. What is "lowbush moose"? Rabbit; highbush moose is the other kind, the big one. Mixed in with the recipes are the stories behind them: the Indian who jogged with a caribou herd, the mess hall that made a delight out of cannery work, the joy of a 10-year-old boy (Nelson) catching a 279-pound halibut from an 8-foot punt.

————. *Smokehouse Bear: More Alaskan Recipes and Stories*, 1982. Gordon Nelson serves up a generous helping of family recipes collected by four generations of Alaska Nelsons, well-seasoned with his vast good humor and penchant for spinning a yarn. Start with any story, any recipe—even smoked bear—and you'll dish up a winner.

————. *Tired Wolf, and the Recipes He Pursued*, 1985. Nelson, now a "Tired Wolf," serves up a new store of recipes to tempt you, all wrapped up in Nelson's wonderfully colorful style of writing.

————. *Hibrow Cow: More Alaskan Stories and Recipes from Gordon R. Nelson*, 1989. This cookbook is Nelson's third encore to his *Lowbush Moose*, with its amusing reminiscences of life in Alaska and its irresistible recipes. What the heck is a Hibrow Cow? Nelson makes it a generic term for sources of animal protein, both game and domestic. Also included are recipes for seafood, eggs, pasta, salads, and breads.

Nims, Cynthia. *Crab (Northwest Homegrown Cookbook Series)*, 2002. Celebrated Seattle-based food writer and chef Cynthia Nims kicks off this series of cookbooks with a tribute to Northwest crab—Dungeness, king, and snow crab—from Alaska to Santa Barbara. Woven through the delectable recipes, Nims shares her special insights about crab and crabbing. Try her Crab and Leek Quiche or Crab and Italian Sausage Cioppino.

————. *Wild Mushrooms (Northwest Homegrown Cookbook Series)*, 2004. Nims continues the series with a tribute to Northwest wild mushrooms—the delectable wild edibles craved by mushroom lovers throughout the world. With as many as 50 edible species of wild mushrooms growing in the ideal Pacific Northwest Coast habitat, Nims has created inspiring recipes, such as Sesame Steak Salad with Soy-Glazed Oyster Mushrooms and Chanterelle and Chicken Pot Pie.

————. *Salmon (Northwest Homegrown Cookbook Series)*, 2005. Nothing represents the bounty of Alaska more than wild Pacific salmon. This book holds Nims's picks for delicious recipes, all featuring the delectable flavor of wild salmon. She also includes many interesting bits of regional salmon history and lore. Delight in her Hot Artichoke and Salmon Dip, Asparagus Soup with Salmon, or Lemon Pasta Alfredo with Salmon.

Persons, Bob, and Deanna. *The Double Musky Inn Cookbook: Alaska's Mountain Cajun Cuisine*, 2006. Named one of the top 10 restaurants in America by the Food Network's Jill Cordes, the Double Musky Inn serves the finest steak and seafood, with an emphasis on spices and seasonings with a New Orleans accent. Mouthwatering specialties are the French Pepper Steak, J.P.'s Cajun Crab Cakes, and Double Musky Chocolate Cake.

Other Books

Cox, Loretta Outwater. *The Storytellers' Club*, 2005. In the dark months of the Far North in the 1920s, a group of Inupiat Eskimo women meet regularly to tell stories. This book is based on the true, compelling tales kept alive through the oral histories of the author's ancestors.

————. *The Winter Walk*, 2003. This tragic yet triumphant story of a young Inupiat mother's winter journey to the Bering Sea coast with her two young children is retold by her great-granddaughter through powerful, haunting narrative.

Fine, Doug. *Not Really an Alaskan Mountain Man*, 2004. East Coast big-city guy, world-traveler, journalist, and otherwise politically savvy Doug Fine settles down in rural Alaska, where men are many and manly, and women with survival skills are good to count among your friends. It's survival of the funniest with Fine as hapless narrator.

Ford, Corey. *Where the Sea Breaks Its Back*, 1992. Author Corey Ford documents the moving story of naturalist Georg Steller, who served on the 1741–42 Russian Alaska expedition with explorer Vitus Bering.

Frederic, Lisa. *Running with Champions*, 2006. Lisa Frederic first fell in love widream about the Far North.

Huntington, Sidney, with Jim Rearden. *Shadows on the Koyukuk*, 1993. In his dramatic autobiography, Alaskan elder Sidney Huntington, half white, half Athabascan, recounts the amazing adventures, heartrending tragedies, and ultimate successes of his long and fascinating life.

Keith, Sam, from the journals and photographs of Richard Proenneke. *One Man's Wilderness*, 1973. Since the 1970s, this best-selling book has touched the hearts and minds of readers all over the world. In midlife, Dick Proenneke left civilization to live alone in Alaska's wilderness, building his own cabin and making what he needed from materials available. Thousands have had such dreams, but Dick Proenneke lived them.

Kremers, Carolyn. *Place of the Pretend People*, 1996. This stunning collection of essays was written by a teacher reflecting on her changed life in the remote Yup'ik Eskimo village of Tununak.

Murie, Margaret. *Two in the Far North*, 1978. This award-winning classic tells the intriguing story about environmentalists Margaret and Olaus Murie.

Rozell, Ned. *Walking My Dog, Jane*, 2000. This story is Rozell's tribute to his adopted state and to the travel partner who carried Rozell's heart, and her own backpack, during a summer spent walking the 800-mile length of the trans-Alaska pipeline.

Sherwonit, Bill. *To the Top of Denali*, 1990. This collection of classic adventure stories brings to life the heroism, triumph, and tragedy of climbing North America's highest peak.

Whitekeys, Mr. *Mr. Whitekeys' Alaska Bizarre*, 1995. A low-falutin' look at the biggest, wildest state in the union, from the originator of the Fly By Night Club's zany musicomedy show.

Index

Photo Credits

AMRC: Rasmuson Center, Anchorage Museum of History and Art.

ASL: Alaska State Library.

UAF: Archives, Alaska and Polar Regions Collections, Rasmuson Library, University of Alaska Fairbanks.

UAA: Archives and Special Collections Department, University of Alaska Anchorage.

Cover and page 1: Alaska Northwest Books Property, courtesy of Inez Schmuland.

p. 7: © Richard Proenneke, *One Man's Wilderness* (Portland, Ore.: Alaska Northwest Books, 1999).

p. 10: UAF, Lawyer and Cora Rivenburg Photograph Collection, 1994-70-266.

p. 9: Seward Community Library Association, Elsie Blue Collection, 15-75.

p. 20: ASL, Mary Nan Gamble Collection, P270-718.

p. 24: UAF, Cordelia L. M. Noble Collection, 1973-203-31.

p. 33: AMRC, Ward W. Wells Collection, www-5076-3.

p. 44: UAF, Albert Johnson Photograph Collection, 1989-0166-401.

p. 50: UAF, Albert Johnson Photograph Collection, 1989-0166-191.

p. 55: UAF, Lawyer and Cora Rivenburg Photograph Collection, 1994-70-98.

p. 65: Consortium Library of the UAA, Ann and Robert Mounteer (Alaska Historical Society Collection) Papers, HMC-0015q.

p. 66: AMRC, Wien Collection, b-85-27-1354.

p. 84: AMRC, Ward W. Wells Collection, www-19-1.

p. 96: UAF, Selid Bassoc Collection, 1964-92-557.

p. 107: AMRC, John Urban Collection, b-64-1-783.

p. 109: ASL, William R. Norton Photographs, W. H. Case, P226-195.

p. 116: AMRC, Wien Collection, b-85-27-1469.

p. 126: ASL, Evelyn Butler and George Dale Collection, George Dale, P306-0811.

p. 130: AMRC, Ward W. Wells Collection, wws-4827-123.

p. 148: UAF, Albert Johnson Photograph Collection, 1989-166-103.

p. 153: ASL, Harry T. Becker Collection, Harry T. Becker, P67-197.

p. 154: AMRC, O. D. Goetze Collection, b01-41-267.

p. 164: AMRC, John Urban Collection, b-64-1-735.

p. 166: AMRC, Crary-Henderson Collection, b62-1-569.

p. 171: AMRC, General Photograph File, b-63-16-80.

p. 174: UAF, Tetlin Photograph Collection, 1987-0114-37.

p. 176: AMRC, Alaska Engineering Commission Collection, aec-g999.

p. 188: UAF, Albert Johnson Photograph Collection, 1989-0166-95.

p. 193: Alaska Northwest Books Property, courtesy of Inez Schmuland.

p. 194: AMRC, John Urban Collection, b-64-1-814.

Printed in the USA
CPSIA information can be obtained
at www.ICGtesting.com
JSHW012027140824
68134JS00033B/2911